50 Canadian Restaurant Dessert Recipes for Home

By: Kelly Johnson

Table of Contents

- Butter Tart
- Nanaimo Bars
- Maple Pecan Pie
- Beavertails
- Bannock
- Saskatoon Berry Pie
- Peameal Bacon Cheesecake
- Nanaimo Bar Cheesecake
- Canadian Maple Cream Pie
- Blueberry Grunt
- Wild Berry Cobbler
- Maple Crème Brûlée
- Tourtière with Apple and Pear Filling
- Maple Sugar Pie
- Lemon Butter Tarts
- Caramel Corn Pudding
- Canadian Butter Pecan Ice Cream
- Red Velvet Cake with Maple Frosting
- Maple Shortbread Cookies
- Apple Fritter Bread Pudding
- Sweet Potato Pie
- Maple-Glazed Donuts
- Berry Rhubarb Crisp
- Classic Pouding Chinois
- Cranberry Walnut Cake
- Maple Walnut Brownies
- Mocha Maple Mousse
- Maple Glazed Cheesecake
- Pumpkin Chiffon Pie
- Apple Cinnamon Roll Casserole
- Chocolate Maple Torte
- Raspberry Lemon Bars

- Maple Butter Cake
- Cinnamon Sugar Beignets
- Blueberry Lemon Cheesecake Bars
- Maple Walnut Fudge
- Sour Cherry Pie
- Vanilla Bean Ice Cream with Maple Syrup
- Pumpkin Spice Cake
- Maple Syrup Panna Cotta
- Chocolate and Maple Pots de Crème
- Maple Bacon Cupcakes
- Strawberry Rhubarb Pie
- Oatmeal Raisin Cookies with Maple Glaze
- Butterscotch Maple Blondies
- Pecan Pie Bars
- Maple-Almond Cake
- Apple Maple Muffins
- Maple Marshmallow Rice Krispies Treats
- Hazelnut Maple Tart

Butter Tart

Ingredients

For the Pastry:

- 1 1/2 cups all-purpose flour
- 1/4 cup granulated sugar
- 1/2 cup unsalted butter (cold, cut into small pieces)
- 1 large egg yolk
- 2-3 tablespoons ice water

For the Filling:

- 1 cup packed brown sugar
- 1/2 cup unsalted butter (softened)
- 1/4 cup corn syrup
- 2 large eggs
- 1 teaspoon vanilla extract
- 1/2 cup raisins or pecans (optional)

Instructions

1. **Prepare the Pastry:**
   - In a large bowl, mix the flour and granulated sugar.
   - Cut in the cold butter using a pastry cutter or your fingers until the mixture resembles coarse crumbs.
   - Stir in the egg yolk. Gradually add the ice water, a tablespoon at a time, until the dough comes together.
   - Gather the dough into a ball, wrap it in plastic wrap, and chill in the refrigerator for at least 30 minutes.
2. **Prepare the Filling:**
   - In a medium bowl, beat together the brown sugar, softened butter, corn syrup, eggs, and vanilla extract until smooth and well combined.
   - If using, fold in the raisins or pecans.
3. **Assemble and Bake:**
   - Preheat your oven to 375°F (190°C).
   - On a lightly floured surface, roll out the chilled dough to about 1/8-inch thickness. Cut into rounds and fit into a 12-cup muffin tin, pressing the dough into the bottom and sides of each cup.
   - Spoon the filling evenly into each pastry-lined cup.
   - Bake for 20-25 minutes, or until the filling is set and the tops are golden brown.
4. **Cool and Serve:**
   - Allow the butter tarts to cool in the tin for about 10 minutes before transferring them to a wire rack to cool completely.

Tips

- **Crust:** For a more tender crust, be careful not to overwork the dough and keep the ingredients cold.
- **Filling:** The filling should be slightly jiggly in the center when done; it will set further as it cools.
- **Variations:** You can experiment with different nuts or add a touch of sea salt on top of the filling before baking for extra flavor.

Butter Tarts are a quintessential Canadian dessert that's sweet, buttery, and irresistible. Enjoy them with a cup of coffee or tea for a delightful treat.

Nanaimo Bars

Ingredients

For the Base Layer:

- **1/2 cup unsalted butter** (softened)
- **1/4 cup granulated sugar**
- **2 tablespoons cocoa powder**
- **2 cups graham cracker crumbs**
- **1 cup shredded coconut**

For the Custard Layer:

- **2 tablespoons unsalted butter** (softened)
- **2 cups powdered sugar**
- **2 tablespoons vanilla custard powder** (or instant vanilla pudding mix)
- **2 tablespoons milk**

For the Top Layer:

- **4 ounces semi-sweet chocolate** (chopped)
- **2 tablespoons unsalted butter**

Instructions

1. **Prepare the Base Layer:**
   - In a medium bowl, cream together the softened butter and granulated sugar until light and fluffy.
   - Stir in the cocoa powder until well combined.
   - Mix in the graham cracker crumbs and shredded coconut.
   - Press the mixture firmly into the bottom of a greased 9x9-inch baking dish to form an even layer.
2. **Prepare the Custard Layer:**
   - In a separate bowl, beat together the softened butter and powdered sugar until smooth.
   - Mix in the vanilla custard powder and milk until the custard is smooth and spreadable.
   - Spread the custard layer evenly over the base layer in the baking dish.
3. **Prepare the Top Layer:**
   - In a small saucepan, melt the chopped chocolate and butter over low heat, stirring constantly until smooth and combined.
   - Pour the chocolate mixture over the custard layer and spread it evenly.

4. **Chill and Serve:**
   - Refrigerate the bars for at least 2 hours, or until the layers are firm and set.
   - Once set, cut into squares and serve.

Tips

- **Custard Powder:** If you can't find vanilla custard powder, instant vanilla pudding mix can be used as a substitute.
- **Cutting Bars:** To get clean cuts, use a sharp knife and wipe it between cuts to prevent sticking.
- **Storage:** Nanaimo Bars should be stored in the refrigerator and will keep well for up to a week.

Nanaimo Bars are a delightful treat with a rich combination of flavors and textures. They are perfect for parties, holiday gatherings, or any time you want to indulge in a sweet, creamy dessert. Enjoy!

Maple Pecan Pie

Ingredients

For the Pie Crust:

- 1 1/4 cups all-purpose flour
- 1/4 teaspoon salt
- 1/4 cup granulated sugar
- 1/2 cup unsalted butter (cold, cut into small pieces)
- 1 large egg yolk
- 2-3 tablespoons ice water

For the Filling:

- 1 cup pure maple syrup
- 1 cup packed brown sugar
- 1/2 cup unsalted butter (softened)
- 4 large eggs
- 1 tablespoon all-purpose flour
- 1 teaspoon vanilla extract
- 1 1/2 cups pecan halves

Instructions

1. **Prepare the Pie Crust:**
     - In a large bowl, combine the flour, salt, and granulated sugar.
     - Cut in the cold butter using a pastry cutter or your fingers until the mixture resembles coarse crumbs.
     - Stir in the egg yolk and add the ice water, a tablespoon at a time, until the dough comes together.
     - Gather the dough into a ball, flatten it into a disk, wrap it in plastic wrap, and refrigerate for at least 30 minutes.
2. **Prepare the Filling:**
     - Preheat your oven to 350°F (175°C).
     - In a medium bowl, whisk together the maple syrup, brown sugar, and softened butter until smooth.
     - Beat in the eggs, one at a time, mixing well after each addition.
     - Stir in the flour and vanilla extract.
     - Fold in the pecan halves.
3. **Assemble and Bake:**
     - On a lightly floured surface, roll out the chilled dough to fit a 9-inch pie dish. Transfer the dough to the pie dish and trim any excess.

- Pour the filling into the prepared pie crust.
- Bake for 50-60 minutes, or until the filling is set and the top is golden brown. The filling will be slightly jiggly in the center; it will firm up as it cools.

4. **Cool and Serve:**
    - Allow the pie to cool completely on a wire rack before slicing.
    - Serve at room temperature or slightly warmed.

Tips

- **Crust:** To prevent the crust from over-browning, you can cover the edges with aluminum foil during baking if needed.
- **Pecans:** For an extra touch, you can toast the pecans lightly before adding them to the filling.
- **Storage:** Store the pie in an airtight container at room temperature for up to 3 days, or refrigerate for longer storage.

Maple Pecan Pie offers a delightful balance of sweet and nutty flavors with the unique richness of maple syrup. It's a perfect dessert for holiday gatherings, special occasions, or whenever you want to enjoy a comforting, homemade treat.

Beavertails

Ingredients

For the Dough:

- **2 1/4 teaspoons (1 packet) active dry yeast**
- **1/4 cup warm water** (about 110°F/45°C)
- **1/4 cup granulated sugar**
- **1/2 cup whole milk** (warm)
- **1 large egg**
- **3 tablespoons unsalted butter** (softened)
- **3 1/2 cups all-purpose flour**
- **1/2 teaspoon salt**

For Frying:

- **Vegetable oil** (for frying)

For Topping (optional):

- **Cinnamon sugar** (1/2 cup granulated sugar mixed with 2 teaspoons ground cinnamon)
- **Chocolate sauce**
- **Maple syrup**
- **Whipped cream**
- **Fruit preserves**

Instructions

1. **Prepare the Dough:**
    - In a small bowl, dissolve the yeast in warm water and let it sit for about 5 minutes, or until foamy.
    - In a large mixing bowl, combine the sugar, warm milk, and yeast mixture.
    - Add the egg and softened butter, mixing until well combined.
    - Gradually add the flour and salt, stirring until the dough starts to come together.
    - Turn the dough out onto a floured surface and knead for about 5-7 minutes, or until smooth and elastic.
    - Place the dough in a lightly greased bowl, cover with a damp cloth, and let it rise in a warm place for about 1 hour, or until doubled in size.
2. **Shape and Fry:**
    - Punch down the risen dough and turn it out onto a floured surface.
    - Roll out the dough to about 1/4-inch thickness. Cut the dough into oval shapes, resembling beaver tails, using a knife or a cookie cutter.

- Heat about 2 inches of vegetable oil in a deep skillet or fryer to 350°F (175°C).
- Fry the dough ovals in batches, for about 1-2 minutes per side, or until golden brown and crispy.
- Remove from the oil with a slotted spoon and drain on paper towels.

3. **Add Toppings:**
   - While still warm, sprinkle the Beavertails with cinnamon sugar or drizzle with chocolate sauce, maple syrup, or your favorite toppings.
4. **Serve:**
   - Serve warm, and enjoy the crispy, sweet treat with your preferred toppings.

Tips

- **Oil Temperature:** Ensure the oil is at the right temperature to avoid soggy Beavertails. If the oil is too hot, the dough will brown too quickly; if too cool, the dough will absorb too much oil.
- **Topping Variety:** Feel free to get creative with your toppings—try fresh fruit, nuts, or even ice cream for a decadent twist.
- **Dough Handling:** If the dough is too sticky, add a little more flour as needed.

Beavertails are a delightful treat perfect for any occasion, offering a crispy exterior and a soft, airy interior with endless topping possibilities. Enjoy making and sharing this iconic Canadian dessert!

Bannock

Ingredients

- **2 cups all-purpose flour**
- **1/4 cup granulated sugar** (optional, for a slightly sweet version)
- **1 tablespoon baking powder**
- **1/2 teaspoon salt**
- **1/4 cup unsalted butter** (cold, cut into small pieces)
- **3/4 cup milk** (adjust as needed for dough consistency)

Instructions

1. **Prepare the Dough:**
    - In a large bowl, whisk together the flour, sugar (if using), baking powder, and salt.
    - Cut in the cold butter using a pastry cutter or your fingers until the mixture resembles coarse crumbs.
    - Gradually add the milk, stirring until the dough comes together. You may need slightly more or less milk depending on the flour.
2. **Choose Your Cooking Method:**
For Baking:
    - Preheat your oven to 400°F (200°C).
    - Transfer the dough to a lightly floured surface and knead gently for about 1 minute.
    - Shape the dough into a round or rectangle and place it on a baking sheet lined with parchment paper.
    - Bake for 20-25 minutes, or until the bread is golden brown and a toothpick inserted into the center comes out clean.
3. **For Frying:**
    - Heat a small amount of oil or butter in a skillet over medium heat.
    - Divide the dough into smaller pieces or flatten it into rounds.
    - Fry each piece for about 3-4 minutes per side, or until golden brown and cooked through.
4. **For Campfire Cooking:**
    - Shape the dough into flat rounds or strips.
    - Wrap the dough around a stick or place it on a hot, greased griddle or flat rock over the campfire.
    - Cook, turning occasionally, until golden brown and cooked through.
5. **Serve:**
    - Allow the bannock to cool slightly before slicing.
    - Serve warm with butter, jam, honey, or as a side to your meal.

Tips

- **Texture:** Avoid over-kneading the dough to ensure a tender texture.
- **Flavor Variations:** Add herbs, cheese, or dried fruit to the dough for different flavors.
- **Storage:** Store leftover bannock in an airtight container at room temperature for a few days, or freeze for longer storage.

Bannock is a versatile and easy-to-make bread that has a comforting, rustic quality. It's perfect for casual gatherings, outdoor adventures, or as a hearty side to any meal. Enjoy experimenting with this traditional recipe!

Saskatoon Berry Pie

Ingredients

For the Pie Crust:

- 2 1/2 cups all-purpose flour
- **1 cup unsalted butter** (cold, cut into small pieces)
- 1/4 cup granulated sugar
- 1/4 teaspoon salt
- 1 large egg yolk
- 2-4 tablespoons ice water

For the Filling:

- 4 cups fresh or frozen Saskatoon berries
- 1 cup granulated sugar
- 1/4 cup all-purpose flour
- 2 tablespoons lemon juice
- 1/2 teaspoon ground cinnamon
- 1/4 teaspoon salt
- **1 tablespoon unsalted butter** (cut into small pieces)

For the Top Crust:

- **1 egg** (beaten, for egg wash)
- **1 tablespoon granulated sugar** (for sprinkling)

Instructions

1. **Prepare the Pie Crust:**
    - In a large bowl, combine the flour, sugar, and salt.
    - Cut in the cold butter using a pastry cutter or your fingers until the mixture resembles coarse crumbs.
    - Stir in the egg yolk and gradually add the ice water, a tablespoon at a time, until the dough comes together.
    - Divide the dough into two equal portions, flatten into disks, and wrap in plastic wrap. Chill in the refrigerator for at least 30 minutes.
2. **Prepare the Filling:**
    - In a large bowl, combine the Saskatoon berries, sugar, flour, lemon juice, cinnamon, and salt. Toss gently to coat the berries evenly.
3. **Assemble the Pie:**
    - Preheat your oven to 375°F (190°C).

- On a lightly floured surface, roll out one disk of dough to fit a 9-inch pie dish. Transfer the rolled dough to the pie dish, pressing it into the bottom and sides.
- Pour the berry filling into the pie crust. Dot with small pieces of butter.
- Roll out the second disk of dough and place it over the filling. You can either cover with a full crust or create a lattice pattern.
- Trim and crimp the edges of the dough to seal the pie. Cut a few small slits in the top crust for steam to escape.
- Brush the top crust with the beaten egg and sprinkle with granulated sugar.

4. **Bake the Pie:**
   - Bake for 50-60 minutes, or until the crust is golden brown and the filling is bubbling. If the crust begins to brown too quickly, cover the edges with aluminum foil.
5. **Cool and Serve:**
   - Allow the pie to cool completely on a wire rack before slicing. This helps the filling to set.

Tips

- **Crust:** For a flakier crust, ensure the butter and water are very cold.
- **Filling:** If using frozen Saskatoon berries, don't thaw them before adding to the pie; this helps prevent a soggy filling.
- **Serving:** Serve warm or at room temperature, optionally with a scoop of vanilla ice cream or a dollop of whipped cream.

Saskatoon Berry Pie is a wonderful way to enjoy the unique flavor of these berries. It's perfect for summer gatherings, holiday dinners, or simply as a special treat to enjoy year-round.

Peameal Bacon Cheesecake

Ingredients

For the Crust:

- 1 1/2 cups graham cracker crumbs
- 1/4 cup granulated sugar
- 1/2 cup unsalted butter (melted)

For the Cheesecake Filling:

- 2 (8-ounce) packages cream cheese (softened)
- 1 cup sour cream
- 1 cup granulated sugar
- 1/2 cup heavy cream
- 3 large eggs
- 1 teaspoon vanilla extract

For the Peameal Bacon Topping:

- 8 ounces peameal bacon (also known as Canadian bacon, diced)
- 1 tablespoon maple syrup (optional, for glazing)

Instructions

1. **Prepare the Crust:**
   - Preheat your oven to 325°F (165°C).
   - In a medium bowl, combine the graham cracker crumbs, granulated sugar, and melted butter. Mix until the crumbs are evenly coated.
   - Press the mixture firmly into the bottom of a 9-inch springform pan to form an even crust. Bake for 10 minutes, then remove from the oven and let cool.
2. **Prepare the Cheesecake Filling:**
   - In a large bowl, beat the softened cream cheese with an electric mixer until smooth and creamy.
   - Add the sour cream and granulated sugar, and continue to beat until well combined.
   - Gradually mix in the heavy cream, followed by the eggs one at a time, beating well after each addition.
   - Stir in the vanilla extract until the mixture is smooth.
3. **Cook the Peameal Bacon:**
   - In a skillet over medium heat, cook the diced peameal bacon until crispy. Drain on paper towels.

- If desired, toss the cooked bacon with maple syrup for a touch of sweetness.
4. **Assemble the Cheesecake:**
    - Pour the cheesecake filling over the pre-baked crust in the springform pan.
    - Gently fold the cooked peameal bacon into the filling, or sprinkle it evenly on top for a more decorative presentation.
5. **Bake the Cheesecake:**
    - Bake the cheesecake for 50-60 minutes, or until the center is set and the edges are lightly golden. The center should still have a slight jiggle when you gently shake the pan.
    - Turn off the oven and let the cheesecake cool in the oven with the door slightly ajar for about 1 hour. This helps prevent cracking.
6. **Chill and Serve:**
    - Remove the cheesecake from the oven and refrigerate for at least 4 hours, or overnight, to fully set.
    - Release the cheesecake from the springform pan and transfer to a serving plate.
    - Garnish with additional crispy peameal bacon if desired.

Tips

- **Bacon:** For a crispier texture, ensure the peameal bacon is well-cooked and drained. You can also cook the bacon in advance and store it in the refrigerator until ready to use.
- **Crust:** For added flavor, you can mix a bit of cinnamon or nutmeg into the graham cracker crust.
- **Serving:** This cheesecake pairs well with a simple green salad or as part of a larger brunch spread.

Peameal Bacon Cheesecake is a savory-sweet creation that's sure to impress your guests and add a unique twist to your dessert repertoire. Enjoy this fusion of flavors and textures in every creamy,

Nanaimo Bar Cheesecake

Ingredients

For the Crust:

- **1 1/2 cups graham cracker crumbs**
- **1/4 cup granulated sugar**
- **1/2 cup unsalted butter** (melted)

For the Custard Layer:

- **1/2 cup unsalted butter** (softened)
- **2 cups powdered sugar**
- **2 tablespoons vanilla custard powder** (or instant vanilla pudding mix)
- **2 tablespoons milk**

For the Cheesecake Filling:

- **2 (8-ounce) packages cream cheese** (softened)
- **1 cup granulated sugar**
- **1 cup sour cream**
- **1 teaspoon vanilla extract**
- **3 large eggs**
- **1 cup heavy cream**

For the Chocolate Ganache:

- **1 cup semi-sweet chocolate chips**
- **1/2 cup heavy cream**

Instructions

1. **Prepare the Crust:**
   - Preheat your oven to 325°F (165°C).
   - In a medium bowl, combine the graham cracker crumbs, granulated sugar, and melted butter. Mix until the crumbs are evenly coated.
   - Press the mixture firmly into the bottom of a 9-inch springform pan to form an even crust. Bake for 10 minutes, then remove from the oven and let cool.
2. **Prepare the Custard Layer:**
   - In a medium bowl, beat together the softened butter and powdered sugar until smooth and creamy.
   - Mix in the vanilla custard powder and milk until the custard mixture is smooth and spreadable.

- Spread the custard layer evenly over the cooled graham cracker crust. Refrigerate while you prepare the cheesecake filling.

3. **Prepare the Cheesecake Filling:**
   - In a large bowl, beat the softened cream cheese and granulated sugar until smooth and creamy.
   - Add the sour cream and vanilla extract, and continue to beat until well combined.
   - Gradually mix in the eggs, one at a time, beating well after each addition.
   - Stir in the heavy cream until the mixture is smooth and well combined.
   - Pour the cheesecake filling over the custard layer in the springform pan, smoothing the top with a spatula.

4. **Bake the Cheesecake:**
   - Bake the cheesecake for 50-60 minutes, or until the center is set and the edges are lightly golden. The center should still have a slight jiggle when you gently shake the pan.
   - Turn off the oven and let the cheesecake cool in the oven with the door slightly ajar for about 1 hour to help prevent cracking.
   - Remove the cheesecake from the oven and refrigerate for at least 4 hours, or overnight, to fully set.

5. **Prepare the Chocolate Ganache:**
   - In a small saucepan, heat the heavy cream over medium heat until it begins to simmer. Remove from heat and add the chocolate chips.
   - Let the mixture sit for 2-3 minutes, then stir until smooth and glossy.
   - Allow the ganache to cool slightly before pouring it over the set cheesecake.

6. **Assemble and Serve:**
   - Spread the chocolate ganache evenly over the chilled cheesecake, smoothing it out with a spatula.
   - Refrigerate the cheesecake for an additional hour to allow the ganache to set.
   - Release the cheesecake from the springform pan and transfer to a serving plate.

Tips

- **Crust:** Press the crust mixture firmly into the pan to ensure it holds together well.
- **Ganache:** For a shinier finish, you can add a small pinch of sea salt to the ganache.
- **Serving:** Let the cheesecake sit at room temperature for about 10-15 minutes before slicing for easier cutting.

Nanaimo Bar Cheesecake combines the best elements of the beloved Canadian dessert into a creamy, luxurious cheesecake that's perfect for special occasions or whenever you want to treat yourself to something extraordinary. Enjoy!

Canadian Maple Cream Pie

Ingredients

For the Pie Crust:

- 1 1/4 cups all-purpose flour
- 1/4 cup granulated sugar
- 1/2 teaspoon salt
- **1/2 cup unsalted butter** (cold, cut into small pieces)
- 1 large egg yolk
- 2-4 tablespoons ice water

For the Maple Cream Filling:

- **1 cup pure maple syrup**
- **1/2 cup heavy cream**
- **1/4 cup granulated sugar**
- **3 large eggs**
- **2 tablespoons all-purpose flour**
- **1 teaspoon vanilla extract**
- **1 tablespoon unsalted butter** (softened)

For Topping:

- **1 cup heavy cream** (whipped, for topping)
- **2 tablespoons pure maple syrup** (for drizzling)
- **1/4 cup chopped toasted pecans or walnuts** (optional, for garnish)

Instructions

1. **Prepare the Pie Crust:**
    - Preheat your oven to 375°F (190°C).
    - In a large bowl, combine the flour, sugar, and salt.
    - Cut in the cold butter using a pastry cutter or your fingers until the mixture resembles coarse crumbs.
    - Stir in the egg yolk and add the ice water, a tablespoon at a time, until the dough comes together.
    - Gather the dough into a ball, flatten it into a disk, wrap it in plastic wrap, and refrigerate for at least 30 minutes.
    - On a lightly floured surface, roll out the chilled dough to fit a 9-inch pie dish. Transfer the dough to the pie dish and trim any excess. Prick the bottom with a fork to prevent bubbling.

- Line the crust with parchment paper and fill with pie weights or dried beans.
- Bake for 15 minutes, then remove the parchment paper and weights. Bake for an additional 5 minutes or until lightly golden. Allow to cool.

2. **Prepare the Maple Cream Filling:**
    - In a medium saucepan, combine the maple syrup, heavy cream, and granulated sugar. Heat over medium heat until the sugar dissolves and the mixture is warm, but not boiling.
    - In a separate bowl, whisk the eggs, flour, and vanilla extract until smooth.
    - Gradually whisk the warm maple syrup mixture into the egg mixture to temper the eggs.
    - Return the combined mixture to the saucepan and cook over medium heat, stirring constantly, until the mixture thickens and coats the back of a spoon.
    - Remove from heat and stir in the softened butter until fully incorporated.
3. **Assemble the Pie:**
    - Pour the maple cream filling into the cooled pie crust. Smooth the top with a spatula.
    - Refrigerate for at least 4 hours or until the filling is set and firm.
4. **Prepare the Topping:**
    - Whip the heavy cream until stiff peaks form. Spread or pipe the whipped cream over the set pie.
    - Drizzle with additional pure maple syrup and sprinkle with chopped toasted pecans or walnuts, if desired.
5. **Serve:**
    - Slice and serve chilled.

Tips

- **Crust:** For a more flavorful crust, you can add a pinch of cinnamon or nutmeg to the flour mixture.
- **Filling:** Make sure to temper the eggs properly to prevent curdling. Stir constantly while cooking the filling to ensure a smooth texture.
- **Storage:** Store the pie in the refrigerator for up to 3 days. It's best enjoyed chilled.

Canadian Maple Cream Pie is a delectable dessert that highlights the rich flavor of maple syrup, making it a standout choice for any occasion. Enjoy the creamy, sweet, and slightly nutty flavors in every bite!

Blueberry Grunt

Ingredients

For the Blueberry Filling:

- 4 cups fresh or frozen blueberries
- 1 cup granulated sugar
- 2 tablespoons cornstarch
- 1 tablespoon lemon juice
- 1/2 teaspoon vanilla extract
- 1/4 teaspoon salt
- 1/2 cup water

For the Biscuit Topping:

- 2 cups all-purpose flour
- 1/4 cup granulated sugar
- 2 teaspoons baking powder
- 1/2 teaspoon salt
- 1/2 cup unsalted butter (cold, cut into small pieces)
- 3/4 cup milk

Instructions

1. **Prepare the Blueberry Filling:**
   - In a large saucepan, combine the blueberries, sugar, cornstarch, lemon juice, vanilla extract, salt, and water.
   - Cook over medium heat, stirring frequently, until the mixture starts to thicken and the blueberries begin to break down. This should take about 5-7 minutes.
   - Once thickened, remove from heat and set aside.
2. **Prepare the Biscuit Topping:**
   - Preheat your oven to 375°F (190°C).
   - In a large bowl, whisk together the flour, sugar, baking powder, and salt.
   - Cut in the cold butter using a pastry cutter or your fingers until the mixture resembles coarse crumbs.
   - Stir in the milk until just combined; the dough will be slightly sticky.
3. **Assemble the Grunt:**
   - Spoon the blueberry filling into a 9-inch baking dish or oven-safe skillet.
   - Drop spoonfuls of the biscuit dough over the blueberry mixture, covering as much of the surface as possible. The biscuit topping doesn't need to be perfect; it's fine if it's a bit uneven.
4. **Bake:**

- Bake in the preheated oven for 30-35 minutes, or until the biscuit topping is golden brown and the blueberry filling is bubbling.
- If the biscuit topping is browning too quickly, cover with aluminum foil and continue baking until fully cooked.

5. **Serve:**
    - Allow the Blueberry Grunt to cool slightly before serving. It can be enjoyed warm or at room temperature.
    - Serve on its own or with a scoop of vanilla ice cream or a dollop of whipped cream for an extra touch of indulgence.

Tips

- **Berries:** If using frozen blueberries, do not thaw them before adding to the filling mixture. This helps maintain their shape and texture.
- **Consistency:** Adjust the amount of cornstarch depending on the juiciness of your berries. The mixture should be thickened but not overly stiff.
- **Topping:** For a slightly sweeter topping, you can sprinkle a little sugar on top of the biscuit dough before baking.

Blueberry Grunt is a nostalgic and comforting dessert that perfectly highlights the fresh, fruity flavors of blueberries. It's an excellent choice for casual gatherings or as a warm treat to enjoy on a cool evening.

Wild Berry Cobbler

Ingredients

For the Berry Filling:

- **4 cups mixed wild berries** (such as blueberries, raspberries, blackberries, and strawberries, fresh or frozen)
- **1 cup granulated sugar**
- **2 tablespoons cornstarch**
- **1 tablespoon lemon juice**
- **1/2 teaspoon vanilla extract**
- **1/4 teaspoon salt**
- **1/2 cup water**

For the Biscuit Topping:

- **2 cups all-purpose flour**
- **1/4 cup granulated sugar**
- **2 teaspoons baking powder**
- **1/2 teaspoon salt**
- **1/2 cup unsalted butter** (cold, cut into small pieces)
- **3/4 cup milk**

Instructions

1. **Prepare the Berry Filling:**
    - Preheat your oven to 375°F (190°C).
    - In a large saucepan, combine the mixed berries, sugar, cornstarch, lemon juice, vanilla extract, salt, and water.
    - Cook over medium heat, stirring frequently, until the mixture begins to thicken and the berries start to break down. This should take about 5-7 minutes.
    - Remove from heat and pour the berry mixture into a 9-inch baking dish or similar oven-safe dish.
2. **Prepare the Biscuit Topping:**
    - In a large bowl, whisk together the flour, sugar, baking powder, and salt.
    - Cut in the cold butter using a pastry cutter or your fingers until the mixture resembles coarse crumbs.
    - Stir in the milk until just combined; the dough will be slightly sticky.
3. **Assemble the Cobbler:**
    - Drop spoonfuls of the biscuit dough over the berry filling, covering as much of the surface as possible. It's okay if some of the filling peeks through; the dough will spread as it bakes.

- For a touch of sweetness, sprinkle a little extra sugar on top of the biscuit dough before baking, if desired.
4. **Bake:**
    - Bake in the preheated oven for 35-40 minutes, or until the biscuit topping is golden brown and the berry filling is bubbling and thickened.
    - If the biscuit topping is browning too quickly, cover with aluminum foil and continue baking until fully cooked.
5. **Serve:**
    - Allow the cobbler to cool slightly before serving. It can be enjoyed warm or at room temperature.
    - Serve on its own or with a scoop of vanilla ice cream, a dollop of whipped cream, or a drizzle of cream for an extra indulgent treat.

Tips

- **Berry Mix:** Feel free to use any combination of wild berries you prefer. Adjust the amount of sugar based on the sweetness of your berries.
- **Topping:** For a crunchier topping, you can sprinkle the biscuit dough with a little coarse sugar before baking.
- **Storage:** Leftovers can be stored in an airtight container in the refrigerator for up to 3 days. Reheat in the oven to restore some of the crispiness.

Wild Berry Cobbler is a versatile and comforting dessert that brings out the best in seasonal berries. Whether served at a summer picnic or a cozy family gathering, it's sure to be a hit with its perfect balance of juicy fruit and tender biscuit topping. Enjoy!

Maple Crème Brûlée

Ingredients

For the Custard:

- **2 cups heavy cream**
- **1/2 cup pure maple syrup**
- **4 large egg yolks**
- **1/4 cup granulated sugar**
- **1 teaspoon vanilla extract**
- **Pinch of salt**

For the Topping:

- **1/4 cup granulated sugar** (for caramelizing)

Instructions

1. **Preheat the Oven:**
   - Preheat your oven to 325°F (163°C).
2. **Prepare the Custard:**
   - In a medium saucepan, combine the heavy cream and maple syrup. Heat over medium heat until just below boiling, stirring occasionally. Remove from heat.
   - In a separate bowl, whisk together the egg yolks, granulated sugar, vanilla extract, and a pinch of salt until well combined.
   - Gradually add the hot cream mixture to the egg yolks, whisking constantly to prevent curdling. This process is known as tempering.
   - Strain the custard mixture through a fine-mesh sieve into a clean bowl or measuring cup to remove any curdled bits.
3. **Bake the Custard:**
   - Place four to six ramekins (depending on size) in a baking dish.
   - Divide the custard mixture evenly among the ramekins.
   - Carefully pour hot water into the baking dish, halfway up the sides of the ramekins, to create a water bath. This helps ensure even cooking and prevents the custards from curdling.
   - Bake in the preheated oven for 40-45 minutes, or until the custards are set around the edges but still slightly wobbly in the center. A knife inserted into the custard should come out clean.
   - Remove the ramekins from the water bath and let them cool to room temperature. Refrigerate for at least 2 hours, or until well chilled.
4. **Caramelize the Sugar:**

- Just before serving, sprinkle a thin, even layer of granulated sugar over the top of each custard.
- Using a kitchen torch, carefully caramelize the sugar until it forms a crisp, golden-brown crust. If you don't have a kitchen torch, you can place the ramekins under a broiler set to high, keeping a close eye on them to prevent burning.

5. **Serve:**
    - Allow the caramelized sugar to cool and harden for a few minutes before serving.
    - Serve the Maple Crème Brûlée immediately after caramelizing for the best texture and flavor.

Tips

- **Maple Syrup:** Use pure maple syrup for the best flavor. The quality of the syrup will directly impact the taste of the custard.
- **Torch:** If using a kitchen torch, work slowly and evenly to achieve a uniform caramelization. If using a broiler, be vigilant as the sugar can burn quickly.
- **Serving:** Maple Crème Brûlée is best enjoyed fresh after caramelizing the sugar, but the custards can be made a day in advance and stored in the refrigerator until needed.

Maple Crème Brûlée combines the classic elegance of crème brûlée with the rich, distinctive flavor of maple syrup, creating a memorable dessert that's perfect for special occasions or a sophisticated treat any time.

Tourtière with Apple and Pear Filling

Ingredients

For the Pastry:

- 2 1/2 cups all-purpose flour
- 1 teaspoon granulated sugar
- 1 teaspoon salt
- **1 cup unsalted butter** (cold, cut into small pieces)
- **1 large egg** (beaten, for egg wash)
- 1/4 to 1/2 cup ice water

For the Apple and Pear Filling:

- **2 large apples** (peeled, cored, and diced)
- **2 large pears** (peeled, cored, and diced)
- 1/2 cup granulated sugar
- 2 tablespoons all-purpose flour
- 1 teaspoon ground cinnamon
- 1/4 teaspoon ground nutmeg
- 1 tablespoon lemon juice
- 1/4 teaspoon salt

Instructions

1. **Prepare the Pastry:**
    - In a large bowl, whisk together the flour, sugar, and salt.
    - Cut in the cold butter using a pastry cutter or your fingers until the mixture resembles coarse crumbs.
    - Gradually add the ice water, a tablespoon at a time, until the dough comes together. The dough should be moist but not sticky.
    - Divide the dough into two equal portions, shape each into a disk, and wrap in plastic wrap. Refrigerate for at least 30 minutes.
2. **Prepare the Apple and Pear Filling:**
    - In a large bowl, combine the diced apples and pears.
    - Add the granulated sugar, flour, cinnamon, nutmeg, lemon juice, and salt. Mix well to coat the fruit evenly.
3. **Assemble the Tourtière:**
    - Preheat your oven to 375°F (190°C).
    - On a lightly floured surface, roll out one disk of dough to fit a 9-inch pie dish. Transfer the dough to the pie dish and press it into the bottom and sides. Trim any excess dough hanging over the edges.

- Spoon the apple and pear filling into the prepared crust, spreading it out evenly.
- Roll out the second disk of dough and place it over the filling. Trim and crimp the edges to seal the pie.
- Cut a few small slits in the top crust to allow steam to escape. Brush the top with the beaten egg for a golden finish.

4. **Bake:**
    - Place the pie on a baking sheet to catch any drips and bake in the preheated oven for 45-50 minutes, or until the crust is golden brown and the filling is bubbling.
    - If the edges of the crust start to brown too quickly, cover them with aluminum foil to prevent burning.

5. **Cool and Serve:**
    - Allow the tourtière to cool for at least 15 minutes before slicing. This helps the filling set and makes it easier to cut.
    - Serve warm or at room temperature. It can be enjoyed on its own or with a scoop of vanilla ice cream or a dollop of whipped cream for a dessert twist.

Tips

- **Fruit:** For a firmer filling, make sure to cut the apples and pears into evenly sized pieces. Using a mix of firm and slightly softer fruits will give you the best texture.
- **Dough:** If the dough becomes too warm while rolling out, chill it briefly to make it easier to handle.
- **Storage:** The pie can be stored in an airtight container at room temperature for up to 3 days or in the refrigerator for up to a week. Reheat in the oven to restore crispness.

Tourtière with Apple and Pear Filling combines the traditional savory pie with a sweet, fruity twist, making it a unique and delicious addition to any meal or special occasion. Enjoy the harmony of flavors and textures in every bite!

Maple Sugar Pie

Ingredients

For the Pie Crust:

- 1 1/4 cups all-purpose flour
- 1/4 cup granulated sugar
- 1/2 teaspoon salt
- 1/2 cup unsalted butter (cold, cut into small pieces)
- 1 large egg yolk
- 2-4 tablespoons ice water

For the Maple Sugar Filling:

- 1 cup pure maple sugar (or packed brown sugar as a substitute)
- 1 cup heavy cream
- 3 large eggs
- 1/4 cup unsalted butter (melted)
- 1 teaspoon vanilla extract
- 1/4 teaspoon salt

Instructions

1. **Prepare the Pie Crust:**
    - Preheat your oven to 375°F (190°C).
    - In a large bowl, combine the flour, sugar, and salt.
    - Cut in the cold butter using a pastry cutter or your fingers until the mixture resembles coarse crumbs.
    - Stir in the egg yolk and add ice water, a tablespoon at a time, until the dough comes together. The dough should be moist but not sticky.
    - Gather the dough into a ball, flatten it into a disk, wrap in plastic wrap, and refrigerate for at least 30 minutes.
    - On a lightly floured surface, roll out the dough to fit a 9-inch pie dish. Transfer the dough to the dish, pressing it into the bottom and sides. Trim any excess dough hanging over the edges.
    - Prick the bottom of the crust with a fork to prevent bubbling. Line with parchment paper and fill with pie weights or dried beans.
    - Bake for 15 minutes, then remove the parchment paper and weights. Bake for an additional 5 minutes until lightly golden. Let cool slightly.
2. **Prepare the Maple Sugar Filling:**
    - In a medium saucepan, heat the heavy cream over medium heat until it begins to simmer. Remove from heat.
    - In a large bowl, whisk together the maple sugar (or brown sugar), eggs, melted butter, vanilla extract, and salt until smooth.
    - Gradually whisk the warm cream into the sugar mixture until fully combined.
3. **Assemble and Bake the Pie:**

- Pour the maple sugar filling into the pre-baked pie crust.
- Bake in the preheated oven for 40-45 minutes, or until the filling is set and slightly puffed. The center should still be a little jiggly but will firm up as it cools.
- If the edges of the crust start to brown too quickly, cover them with aluminum foil.

4. **Cool and Serve:**
    - Allow the pie to cool completely before serving. This helps the filling set properly and makes it easier to slice.
    - Serve on its own or with a dollop of whipped cream or a scoop of vanilla ice cream for an extra touch of indulgence.

Tips

- **Maple Sugar:** For the best flavor, use pure maple sugar. If maple sugar is unavailable, packed brown sugar can be used as a substitute, but the flavor will be less intense.
- **Crust:** Ensure the pie crust is well-chilled before baking to prevent shrinking. If it does shrink, gently press it back into place before adding the filling.
- **Storage:** Store leftovers in an airtight container at room temperature for up to 3 days or in the refrigerator for up to a week.

Maple Sugar Pie is a rich and satisfying dessert that perfectly highlights the sweet, distinctive flavor of maple syrup. It's an ideal choice for special occasions or as a comforting treat during the colder months. Enjoy each sweet, creamy bite!

Lemon Butter Tarts

Ingredients

For the Tart Crust:

- **1 1/2 cups all-purpose flour**
- **1/4 cup granulated sugar**
- **1/4 teaspoon salt**
- **1/2 cup unsalted butter** (cold, cut into small pieces)
- **1 large egg yolk**
- **1-2 tablespoons ice water**

For the Lemon Filling:

- **1/2 cup granulated sugar**
- **1/4 cup unsalted butter** (softened)
- **2 large eggs**
- **1/4 cup freshly squeezed lemon juice** (about 1-2 lemons)
- **1 tablespoon lemon zest** (from 1 lemon)
- **1/4 teaspoon salt**

Instructions

1. **Prepare the Tart Crust:**
   - Preheat your oven to 375°F (190°C).
   - In a large bowl, combine the flour, sugar, and salt.
   - Cut in the cold butter using a pastry cutter or your fingers until the mixture resembles coarse crumbs.
   - Stir in the egg yolk and add ice water, a tablespoon at a time, until the dough comes together. The dough should be moist but not sticky.
   - Gather the dough into a ball, flatten it into a disk, wrap in plastic wrap, and refrigerate for at least 30 minutes.
   - On a lightly floured surface, roll out the dough to about 1/8-inch thickness. Cut into circles large enough to fit into a tartlet pan or mini muffin tin.
   - Gently press the dough circles into the tartlet pans, trimming any excess. Prick the bottoms with a fork to prevent bubbling.
   - Chill the tart shells in the refrigerator for 10 minutes before baking.
   - Bake in the preheated oven for 10-12 minutes, or until the edges are lightly golden. Let cool slightly before filling.
2. **Prepare the Lemon Filling:**
   - In a medium bowl, cream together the sugar and softened butter until light and fluffy.
   - Beat in the eggs one at a time, mixing well after each addition.
   - Stir in the lemon juice, lemon zest, and salt until fully combined.
3. **Assemble and Bake the Tarts:**

- Spoon the lemon filling into the pre-baked tart shells, filling them almost to the top.
- Bake in the preheated oven for 15-20 minutes, or until the filling is set and the tops are lightly golden.
- Remove from the oven and allow the tarts to cool completely in the pans before removing.

4. **Serve:**
   - Once cooled, gently remove the tarts from the pans.
   - Dust with powdered sugar, if desired, before serving.
   - Enjoy the tarts on their own or with a dollop of whipped cream for a little extra indulgence.

Tips

- **Crust:** For a more tender crust, handle the dough as little as possible and ensure the butter is very cold.
- **Filling:** If you prefer a smoother filling, you can strain the lemon filling through a fine-mesh sieve before pouring it into the tart shells.
- **Storage:** Store the tarts in an airtight container at room temperature for up to 3 days, or in the refrigerator for up to a week. They can be frozen for up to 2 months.

Lemon Butter Tarts offer a delightful blend of buttery crust and tangy lemon filling, making them a perfect treat for any occasion. Their vibrant flavor and elegant presentation are sure to impress family and friends alike!

Caramel Corn Pudding

Ingredients

For the Caramel Corn:

- **4 cups caramel popcorn** (store-bought or homemade)
- **2 tablespoons unsalted butter**

For the Pudding:

- **2 cups whole milk**
- **1/2 cup granulated sugar**
- **1/4 cup cornstarch**
- **1/4 teaspoon salt**
- **3 large egg yolks**
- **1/4 cup unsalted butter** (cubed)
- **1 teaspoon vanilla extract**
- **1/2 cup caramel sauce** (store-bought or homemade)

For Garnish:

- **Extra caramel corn** (for topping)
- **Additional caramel sauce** (optional, for drizzling)

Instructions

1. **Prepare the Caramel Corn:**
   - If using store-bought caramel popcorn, you can skip this step. If making homemade caramel corn, prepare it according to your recipe and let it cool completely.
   - Once the caramel popcorn is cooled, melt 2 tablespoons of unsalted butter in a large pan over medium heat.
   - Add the caramel popcorn to the pan and toss gently to coat with the melted butter. Set aside to cool.
2. **Prepare the Pudding:**
   - In a medium saucepan, whisk together the milk, sugar, cornstarch, and salt. Cook over medium heat, stirring constantly, until the mixture begins to thicken and bubble.
   - In a separate bowl, whisk the egg yolks. Gradually add a small amount of the hot milk mixture to the egg yolks, whisking constantly to temper them.
   - Return the egg mixture to the saucepan with the remaining milk mixture and continue cooking, stirring constantly, until the pudding thickens further and reaches a pudding-like consistency.
   - Remove from heat and stir in the cubed butter until fully melted and incorporated.
   - Stir in the vanilla extract and caramel sauce until the mixture is smooth and well combined.

3. **Assemble the Pudding:**
   - Allow the pudding to cool slightly before assembling.
   - In serving glasses or bowls, layer the pudding with caramel corn. Start with a layer of pudding, followed by a layer of caramel corn, and repeat as desired.
   - For a decorative touch, reserve some caramel corn to sprinkle on top of each serving.
4. **Chill and Serve:**
   - Refrigerate the pudding for at least 2 hours to allow it to set and for the flavors to meld together.
   - Just before serving, drizzle additional caramel sauce over the top, if desired, and garnish with the reserved caramel corn.

Tips

- **Caramel Corn:** For the best texture, avoid adding the caramel corn until just before serving to maintain its crunchiness. If it sits in the pudding for too long, it may become soggy.
- **Pudding Consistency:** If the pudding thickens too much while cooling, whisk in a little milk to reach your desired consistency before assembling.
- **Caramel Sauce:** Homemade caramel sauce adds a special touch, but store-bought caramel sauce works perfectly as well.

Caramel Corn Pudding is a delightful dessert that combines creamy pudding with the irresistible crunch of caramel corn, offering a sweet and satisfying treat that's perfect for any occasion. Enjoy the layers of flavor and texture in every spoonful!

Canadian Butter Pecan Ice Cream

Ingredients

For the Buttered Pecans:

- 1 cup pecan halves
- 2 tablespoons unsalted butter
- 1/4 cup brown sugar
- Pinch of salt

For the Ice Cream Base:

- 1 cup whole milk
- 1 cup heavy cream
- 3/4 cup granulated sugar
- 1/4 cup pure maple syrup
- 1 teaspoon vanilla extract
- 4 large egg yolks

Instructions

1. **Prepare the Buttered Pecans:**
    - Preheat your oven to 350°F (175°C).
    - In a medium skillet, melt the butter over medium heat. Add the pecan halves and cook, stirring frequently, until they are toasted and fragrant, about 4-5 minutes.
    - Stir in the brown sugar and a pinch of salt. Continue to cook, stirring, until the sugar is melted and the pecans are evenly coated. Remove from heat and spread the pecans on a parchment-lined baking sheet to cool. Once cooled, roughly chop the pecans.
2. **Prepare the Ice Cream Base:**
    - In a medium saucepan, combine the milk, heavy cream, and granulated sugar. Heat over medium heat, stirring occasionally, until the mixture is hot and the sugar is dissolved. Do not let it boil.
    - In a separate bowl, whisk the egg yolks. Gradually add a small amount of the hot milk mixture to the egg yolks, whisking constantly to temper them.
    - Return the egg yolk mixture to the saucepan with the remaining milk mixture, and continue to cook over medium heat, stirring constantly, until the mixture thickens enough to coat the back of a spoon. Do not let it boil.
    - Remove from heat and stir in the pure maple syrup and vanilla extract.
3. **Chill the Mixture:**
    - Pour the ice cream base through a fine-mesh sieve into a clean bowl to strain out any curdled bits.

- Allow the mixture to cool to room temperature. Cover and refrigerate for at least 4 hours or overnight to chill thoroughly.
4. **Churn and Mix:**
    - Once the mixture is well chilled, churn it in an ice cream maker according to the manufacturer's instructions.
    - When the ice cream is nearly done churning, gently fold in the chopped buttered pecans.
5. **Freeze and Serve:**
    - Transfer the churned ice cream to an airtight container and freeze for at least 2 hours, or until firm.
    - Scoop and serve the ice cream directly from the freezer. For a smoother texture, let it sit at room temperature for a few minutes before serving.

Tips

- **Pecans:** For the best flavor, ensure the pecans are toasted and well-coated in butter and sugar. This adds a rich, caramelized note to the ice cream.
- **Ice Cream Maker:** Follow your ice cream maker's instructions for churning times and methods for best results.
- **Storage:** Homemade ice cream is best enjoyed within a couple of weeks. Store it in an airtight container to prevent ice crystals from forming.

Canadian Butter Pecan Ice Cream brings together the rich flavors of buttery, toasted pecans with the smooth, creamy sweetness of maple and vanilla ice cream. It's a delightful treat that's sure to impress and satisfy any ice cream lover.

Red Velvet Cake with Maple Frosting

Ingredients

For the Red Velvet Cake:

- 2 1/2 cups all-purpose flour
- 1 1/2 cups granulated sugar
- 1 teaspoon baking powder
- 1 teaspoon baking soda
- 1 teaspoon salt
- 1 tablespoon unsweetened cocoa powder
- 1 cup vegetable oil
- 1 cup buttermilk (room temperature)
- 2 large eggs (room temperature)
- 2 tablespoons red food coloring
- 1 teaspoon white vinegar
- 1 teaspoon vanilla extract

For the Maple Frosting:

- 1 cup unsalted butter (softened)
- 4 cups powdered sugar
- 1/4 cup pure maple syrup
- 1/4 cup heavy cream
- 1 teaspoon vanilla extract
- Pinch of salt

Instructions

1. **Prepare the Red Velvet Cake:**
    - Preheat your oven to 350°F (175°C). Grease and flour two 9-inch round cake pans, or line them with parchment paper.
    - In a large bowl, sift together the flour, sugar, baking powder, baking soda, salt, and cocoa powder.
    - In another bowl, whisk together the oil, buttermilk, eggs, red food coloring, vinegar, and vanilla extract.
    - Gradually add the wet ingredients to the dry ingredients, mixing until just combined. Be careful not to overmix.
    - Divide the batter evenly between the prepared cake pans and smooth the tops with a spatula.
    - Bake in the preheated oven for 25-30 minutes, or until a toothpick inserted into the center comes out clean.

- Allow the cakes to cool in the pans for 10 minutes before transferring them to a wire rack to cool completely.

2. **Prepare the Maple Frosting:**
   - In a large bowl, beat the softened butter with an electric mixer until creamy and smooth.
   - Gradually add the powdered sugar, mixing on low speed until fully incorporated.
   - Add the maple syrup, heavy cream, vanilla extract, and a pinch of salt. Beat on medium-high speed until the frosting is light and fluffy.
   - If the frosting is too thick, add a bit more cream. If it's too thin, add a bit more powdered sugar to reach your desired consistency.

3. **Assemble the Cake:**
   - Once the cakes are completely cooled, level the tops if necessary using a serrated knife to ensure even layers.
   - Place one layer of cake on a serving plate or cake stand. Spread a generous amount of maple frosting on top.
   - Place the second layer of cake on top of the frosting, and frost the top and sides of the cake with the remaining maple frosting.
   - Smooth the frosting with a spatula or create decorative swirls as desired.

4. **Decorate and Serve:**
   - Decorate the cake with any additional toppings you like, such as crushed pecans or a drizzle of maple syrup.
   - Refrigerate the cake for at least 30 minutes before serving to allow the frosting to set.

Tips

- **Food Coloring:** Adjust the amount of food coloring to achieve your desired shade of red. You can use gel food coloring for a more vibrant hue.
- **Cake Layers:** If the cakes have domed tops, level them carefully to ensure a stable and even cake stack.
- **Frosting Consistency:** Make sure the butter is softened but not melted for the frosting. This helps achieve a creamy texture without being too runny.

Red Velvet Cake with Maple Frosting offers a delectable blend of classic red velvet flavors and the rich, distinctive taste of maple. It's a visually stunning and delicious dessert that's perfect for celebrating special occasions or simply enjoying a treat with loved ones.

Maple Shortbread Cookies

Ingredients

- **1 cup unsalted butter** (softened)
- **1/2 cup granulated sugar**
- **1/4 cup pure maple syrup**
- **1/4 teaspoon salt**
- **2 1/4 cups all-purpose flour**
- **1/2 teaspoon maple extract** (optional, for enhanced maple flavor)
- **Additional granulated sugar** (for sprinkling, optional)

Instructions

1. **Prepare the Dough:**
   - In a large bowl, cream together the softened butter and granulated sugar until light and fluffy.
   - Mix in the pure maple syrup and salt, beating until well combined. If using, add the maple extract and mix thoroughly.
   - Gradually add the all-purpose flour, mixing on low speed until just combined. The dough should be soft and slightly crumbly.
2. **Chill the Dough:**
   - Gather the dough into a ball, flatten it into a disk, and wrap it in plastic wrap. Refrigerate for at least 1 hour or until firm. Chilling the dough helps the cookies hold their shape during baking.
3. **Preheat the Oven:**
   - Preheat your oven to 350°F (175°C). Line baking sheets with parchment paper or silicone baking mats.
4. **Roll and Cut the Cookies:**
   - On a lightly floured surface, roll out the dough to about 1/4-inch thickness. Use cookie cutters to cut out shapes, or simply slice the dough into squares or rectangles.
   - Transfer the cut-out cookies to the prepared baking sheets, spacing them about 1 inch apart. If desired, sprinkle a little granulated sugar on top of each cookie for extra sweetness and a bit of sparkle.
5. **Bake the Cookies:**
   - Bake in the preheated oven for 12-15 minutes, or until the edges are lightly golden. The centers should remain pale.
   - Allow the cookies to cool on the baking sheets for a few minutes before transferring them to a wire rack to cool completely.
6. **Serve:**

- Enjoy the cookies once they are completely cooled. They pair wonderfully with a cup of tea or coffee.

Tips

- **Butter:** Ensure the butter is softened but not melted. This helps in achieving the right texture and consistency in the dough.
- **Maple Syrup:** Use pure maple syrup for the best flavor. Avoid maple-flavored syrups as they lack the depth of flavor.
- **Cutting Shapes:** For cleaner edges, chill the dough again briefly if it becomes too soft while cutting out shapes.

Maple Shortbread Cookies are a perfect blend of buttery richness and maple sweetness. Their simple elegance and delectable flavor make them a delightful treat for any time of year. Enjoy these cookies as a special treat or a charming homemade gift for friends and family!

Apple Fritter Bread Pudding

Ingredients

For the Bread Pudding:

- **1 loaf day-old French bread** (or any sturdy bread), cut into 1-inch cubes
- **2 cups whole milk**
- **1 cup heavy cream**
- **4 large eggs**
- **3/4 cup granulated sugar**
- **1 teaspoon vanilla extract**
- **1 teaspoon ground cinnamon**
- **1/4 teaspoon ground nutmeg**
- **1/2 teaspoon salt**
- **2 medium apples** (peeled, cored, and diced)
- **2 tablespoons unsalted butter** (for sautéing apples)
- **1/4 cup brown sugar** (for apples)

For the Glaze:

- **1 cup powdered sugar**
- **2 tablespoons milk**
- **2 tablespoons pure maple syrup** (or more milk, if needed)
- **1/2 teaspoon vanilla extract**

Instructions

1. **Prepare the Apples:**
   - In a medium skillet, melt the butter over medium heat. Add the diced apples and cook until they begin to soften, about 5 minutes.
   - Stir in the brown sugar and cook for an additional 3-4 minutes, until the apples are tender and caramelized. Remove from heat and set aside.
2. **Prepare the Bread Pudding:**
   - Preheat your oven to 350°F (175°C). Grease a 9x13-inch baking dish or similarly sized casserole dish.
   - In a large bowl, whisk together the milk, heavy cream, eggs, granulated sugar, vanilla extract, cinnamon, nutmeg, and salt until well combined.
   - Add the bread cubes to the mixture and gently stir to coat the bread evenly. Let the mixture sit for about 15 minutes, allowing the bread to soak up the custard mixture.
   - Gently fold in the cooked apples and any caramel sauce from the skillet.
3. **Bake the Bread Pudding:**

- Pour the bread and apple mixture into the prepared baking dish, spreading it evenly.
- Bake in the preheated oven for 45-50 minutes, or until the pudding is set in the center and the top is golden brown. A knife inserted into the center should come out clean.

4. **Prepare the Glaze:**
   - While the bread pudding is baking, prepare the glaze by whisking together the powdered sugar, milk, maple syrup, and vanilla extract in a small bowl. Adjust the consistency with more milk if needed.
5. **Serve:**
   - Allow the bread pudding to cool slightly before drizzling with the glaze. Serve warm or at room temperature.

Tips

- **Bread:** Use day-old bread for the best texture. Fresh bread can become too soggy.
- **Apples:** Any apple variety suitable for baking will work. Granny Smith or Honeycrisp apples are excellent choices.
- **Glaze:** Adjust the thickness of the glaze to your preference. For a thinner glaze, add a little more milk; for a thicker glaze, use less milk.

Apple Fritter Bread Pudding combines the comforting elements of bread pudding with the sweet, spiced flavors of apple fritters, offering a delightful and satisfying dessert that's sure to please any crowd. Enjoy the warm, cinnamon-infused pudding with its luscious apple chunks and sweet glaze for a treat that's both comforting and indulgent.

Sweet Potato Pie

Ingredients

For the Pie Crust:

- **1 1/2 cups all-purpose flour**
- **1/2 cup unsalted butter** (cold and cut into small pieces)
- **1/4 cup granulated sugar**
- **1/4 teaspoon salt**
- **1/4 cup ice water** (more if needed)

For the Sweet Potato Filling:

- **2 cups cooked sweet potato puree** (about 2 medium sweet potatoes)
- **3/4 cup granulated sugar**
- **1/2 cup packed brown sugar**
- **1/2 cup evaporated milk**
- **1/4 cup unsalted butter** (melted)
- **2 large eggs**
- **1 teaspoon vanilla extract**
- **1 teaspoon ground cinnamon**
- **1/2 teaspoon ground nutmeg**
- **1/4 teaspoon ground ginger**
- **1/4 teaspoon salt**

Instructions

1. **Prepare the Pie Crust:**
   - In a large bowl, combine the flour, granulated sugar, and salt. Cut in the cold butter using a pastry blender or your fingers until the mixture resembles coarse crumbs.
   - Gradually add the ice water, one tablespoon at a time, until the dough comes together. Be careful not to add too much water; the dough should be just moist enough to hold together.
   - Form the dough into a disc, wrap it in plastic wrap, and refrigerate for at least 30 minutes.
2. **Prepare the Sweet Potato Filling:**
   - If you haven't already cooked the sweet potatoes, peel and cube them, then boil in water until tender, about 15-20 minutes. Drain and mash until smooth, or use a food processor to make a puree.

- In a large bowl, mix the sweet potato puree with the granulated sugar, brown sugar, evaporated milk, melted butter, eggs, vanilla extract, cinnamon, nutmeg, ginger, and salt. Whisk until smooth and well combined.
3. **Assemble the Pie:**
    - Preheat your oven to 375°F (190°C).
    - On a lightly floured surface, roll out the chilled dough to fit a 9-inch pie pan. Transfer the dough to the pan, pressing it into the bottom and up the sides. Trim any excess dough and crimp the edges if desired.
    - Pour the sweet potato filling into the prepared pie crust, smoothing the top with a spatula.
4. **Bake the Pie:**
    - Bake in the preheated oven for 50-60 minutes, or until the filling is set and a knife inserted into the center comes out clean. The edges of the crust should be golden brown.
    - Allow the pie to cool on a wire rack before serving. This will help the filling to firm up further.
5. **Serve:**
    - Serve the pie at room temperature or chilled. It pairs wonderfully with a dollop of whipped cream or a scoop of vanilla ice cream.

Tips

- **Sweet Potato Puree:** For convenience, you can use canned sweet potato puree, but ensure it's plain and not sweetened or spiced.
- **Pie Crust:** If you prefer, you can use a pre-made pie crust to save time. Just follow the package directions for pre-baking if needed.
- **Spices:** Adjust the spices to your taste. You can add more cinnamon or nutmeg if you prefer a spicier pie.

Sweet Potato Pie is a beloved classic that brings together the creamy sweetness of sweet potatoes with warm spices in a buttery, flaky crust. It's a comforting dessert that's sure to be a hit with family and friends, offering a delicious alternative to pumpkin pie with its unique and satisfying flavor.

Maple-Glazed Donuts

Ingredients

For the Donuts:

- **2 1/4 teaspoons active dry yeast** (1 packet)
- **1/4 cup warm water** (110°F or 45°C)
- **1/4 cup granulated sugar**
- **1/2 cup whole milk**
- **1/4 cup unsalted butter** (softened)
- **2 large eggs**
- **3 1/2 cups all-purpose flour**
- **1/2 teaspoon salt**
- **Vegetable oil** (for frying)

For the Maple Glaze:

- **1 1/2 cups powdered sugar**
- **1/4 cup pure maple syrup**
- **2 tablespoons whole milk**
- **1/2 teaspoon vanilla extract**

Instructions

1. **Prepare the Donut Dough:**
    - In a small bowl, dissolve the yeast in warm water with a pinch of sugar. Let it sit for about 5-10 minutes, or until frothy.
    - In a large mixing bowl, combine the remaining granulated sugar, milk, softened butter, and eggs. Mix until well combined.
    - Add the yeast mixture to the bowl and stir to combine.
    - Gradually add the flour and salt, mixing until a soft dough forms. You may need to add a little more flour if the dough is too sticky.
    - Turn the dough out onto a floured surface and knead for about 5-7 minutes, or until smooth and elastic.
    - Place the dough in a lightly oiled bowl, cover with plastic wrap or a clean cloth, and let it rise in a warm place for about 1-1.5 hours, or until doubled in size.
2. **Shape and Fry the Donuts:**
    - After the dough has risen, punch it down and turn it out onto a floured surface. Roll out the dough to about 1/2-inch thickness.
    - Use a donut cutter or two round cutters (one large and one small for the hole) to cut out donut shapes. Gather and re-roll the scraps to cut additional donuts.

- Place the cut donuts and holes on a floured baking sheet, cover with a cloth, and let them rise for another 30 minutes.
3. **Fry the Donuts:**
   - Heat vegetable oil in a deep fryer or large pot to 350°F (175°C). The oil should be deep enough to submerge the donuts.
   - Fry the donuts in batches, making sure not to overcrowd the pot. Cook each donut for about 1-2 minutes on each side, or until golden brown.
   - Use a slotted spoon to remove the donuts from the oil and transfer them to a paper towel-lined plate to drain.
4. **Prepare the Maple Glaze:**
   - In a medium bowl, whisk together the powdered sugar, maple syrup, milk, and vanilla extract until smooth. Adjust the consistency with more milk or powdered sugar as needed.
5. **Glaze the Donuts:**
   - Once the donuts are slightly cooled but still warm, dip them into the maple glaze, ensuring they are coated evenly.
   - Allow the excess glaze to drip off, then place the glazed donuts on a wire rack to let the glaze set.
6. **Serve:**
   - Enjoy the donuts while they are still fresh and warm. They are perfect on their own or paired with a cup of coffee or tea.

Tips

- **Frying:** Make sure the oil temperature remains consistent. Too hot, and the donuts will burn; too cool, and they will absorb too much oil.
- **Yeast:** Ensure your yeast is fresh and not expired for the best results.
- **Glaze Consistency:** If the glaze is too thick, add a little more milk; if too thin, add more powdered sugar.

Maple-Glazed Donuts offer a sweet, indulgent treat with a deliciously smooth maple glaze that perfectly complements the light, fluffy texture of homemade donuts. They make for a delightful breakfast or a special treat any time of day!

Berry Rhubarb Crisp

Ingredients

For the Filling:

- **3 cups fresh rhubarb** (chopped into 1-inch pieces)
- **2 cups mixed berries** (such as strawberries, blueberries, raspberries, or blackberries, fresh or frozen)
- **3/4 cup granulated sugar**
- **1/4 cup light brown sugar**
- **2 tablespoons cornstarch**
- **1 tablespoon lemon juice**
- **1 teaspoon vanilla extract**
- **1/2 teaspoon ground cinnamon**

For the Crisp Topping:

- **1 cup old-fashioned rolled oats**
- **1/2 cup all-purpose flour**
- **1/2 cup light brown sugar**
- **1/4 teaspoon salt**
- **1/4 teaspoon ground cinnamon**
- **1/2 cup unsalted butter** (cold and cut into small pieces)

Instructions

1. **Prepare the Filling:**
    - Preheat your oven to 350°F (175°C). Grease a 9x13-inch baking dish or similar-sized casserole dish.
    - In a large bowl, combine the chopped rhubarb, mixed berries, granulated sugar, brown sugar, cornstarch, lemon juice, vanilla extract, and cinnamon. Toss gently to coat the fruit evenly.
    - Pour the fruit mixture into the prepared baking dish, spreading it out evenly.
2. **Prepare the Crisp Topping:**
    - In a separate bowl, combine the rolled oats, flour, brown sugar, salt, and cinnamon.
    - Add the cold, cubed butter to the oat mixture. Using a pastry cutter, fork, or your fingers, work the butter into the dry ingredients until the mixture resembles coarse crumbs with pea-sized pieces of butter.
3. **Assemble and Bake:**
    - Sprinkle the crisp topping evenly over the fruit filling in the baking dish.

- Bake in the preheated oven for 40-45 minutes, or until the topping is golden brown and the filling is bubbly and thickened.
4. **Serve:**
    - Allow the crisp to cool slightly before serving. It can be enjoyed warm, at room temperature, or cold.
    - Serve with a scoop of vanilla ice cream or a dollop of whipped cream for added indulgence.

Tips

- **Fruit:** You can use a variety of berries or even a mix of fresh and frozen fruits. If using frozen berries, there is no need to thaw them; just add them directly to the mixture.
- **Rhubarb:** If you prefer a sweeter filling, you can adjust the amount of sugar to taste. Rhubarb is naturally tart, so more sugar may be needed depending on your preference.
- **Topping:** For a variation, you can add chopped nuts such as pecans or walnuts to the crisp topping for extra crunch and flavor.

Berry Rhubarb Crisp is a perfect dessert for any season, offering a deliciously tangy and sweet filling with a crunchy, buttery topping. It's a comforting treat that's easy to prepare and sure to be enjoyed by family and friends alike.

Classic Pouding Chinois

Ingredients

For the Meat Layer:

- **1 lb (450 g) ground beef**
- **1 small onion** (diced)
- **2 cloves garlic** (minced)
- **1 cup frozen corn kernels** (or fresh corn, if available)
- **1/2 cup beef broth**
- **1 tablespoon tomato paste**
- **1 teaspoon dried thyme**
- **1 teaspoon dried rosemary**
- **1/2 teaspoon salt**
- **1/4 teaspoon black pepper**

For the Mashed Potato Topping:

- **4 large potatoes** (peeled and diced)
- **1/4 cup unsalted butter**
- **1/4 cup whole milk**
- **1/2 teaspoon salt**
- **1/4 teaspoon black pepper**
- **1/4 cup grated cheddar cheese** (optional, for extra flavor)

Instructions

1. **Prepare the Meat Layer:**
    - Preheat your oven to 375°F (190°C).
    - In a large skillet over medium heat, cook the ground beef, onion, and garlic until the meat is browned and the onion is tender, about 5-7 minutes. Drain any excess fat.
    - Stir in the frozen corn, beef broth, tomato paste, thyme, rosemary, salt, and pepper. Cook for an additional 5 minutes, until the mixture is well combined and slightly thickened. Remove from heat.
2. **Prepare the Mashed Potato Topping:**
    - While the meat mixture is cooking, place the diced potatoes in a large pot and cover with water. Bring to a boil and cook until the potatoes are tender, about 15-20 minutes.
    - Drain the potatoes and return them to the pot. Add the butter, milk, salt, and pepper. Mash until smooth and creamy. If desired, stir in the grated cheddar cheese for added flavor.

3. **Assemble the Pouding Chinois:**
   - Spread the meat mixture evenly in the bottom of a 9x13-inch baking dish or similar-sized casserole dish.
   - Spoon the mashed potatoes over the meat layer, spreading them out evenly with a spatula. Use the back of a spoon or a fork to create some texture on the surface of the mashed potatoes.
4. **Bake:**
   - Bake in the preheated oven for 30-35 minutes, or until the mashed potato topping is golden brown and the edges are bubbly.
5. **Serve:**
   - Allow the Pouding Chinois to cool for a few minutes before serving. This dish is delicious on its own or served with a side salad or steamed vegetables.

Tips

- **Variations:** For a different flavor, you can add vegetables such as peas or carrots to the meat layer. Some recipes also include a layer of gravy.
- **Cheese:** Adding cheese to the mashed potato topping is optional but adds a nice richness and extra flavor.
- **Make Ahead:** Pouding Chinois can be assembled ahead of time and stored in the refrigerator for up to 2 days before baking. It can also be frozen for up to 3 months.

Classic Pouding Chinois is a comforting and hearty dish that brings together layers of seasoned ground beef, sweet corn, and creamy mashed potatoes. This Canadian favorite is perfect for family dinners and offers a satisfying, homey meal that's sure to be enjoyed by all.

Cranberry Walnut Cake

Ingredients

For the Cake:

- 1 1/2 cups all-purpose flour
- 1 teaspoon baking powder
- 1/2 teaspoon baking soda
- 1/2 teaspoon salt
- 1/2 cup unsalted butter (softened)
- 1 cup granulated sugar
- 2 large eggs
- 1 teaspoon vanilla extract
- 1/2 cup sour cream
- 1/2 cup milk
- 1 1/2 cups fresh cranberries (or frozen cranberries, thawed and drained)
- 1/2 cup chopped walnuts (toasted if desired)

For the Streusel Topping (Optional):

- 1/3 cup all-purpose flour
- 1/4 cup granulated sugar
- 1/4 cup unsalted butter (cold and cubed)
- 1/4 cup chopped walnuts

For the Glaze (Optional):

- 1/2 cup powdered sugar
- 2 tablespoons orange juice
- 1/2 teaspoon vanilla extract

Instructions

1. **Prepare the Cake Batter:**
   - Preheat your oven to 350°F (175°C). Grease and flour a 9-inch round cake pan or a 9x9-inch square baking dish.
   - In a medium bowl, whisk together the flour, baking powder, baking soda, and salt.
   - In a large bowl, cream the softened butter and granulated sugar together until light and fluffy.
   - Beat in the eggs one at a time, then add the vanilla extract.

- Gradually add the flour mixture to the butter mixture, alternating with the sour cream and milk, beginning and ending with the flour mixture. Mix until just combined.
- Gently fold in the cranberries and chopped walnuts.

2. **Prepare the Streusel Topping (if using):**
   - In a small bowl, combine the flour, granulated sugar, and cold butter. Use a pastry cutter or your fingers to work the butter into the dry ingredients until the mixture resembles coarse crumbs.
   - Stir in the chopped walnuts.

3. **Assemble and Bake:**
   - Pour the batter into the prepared pan and smooth the top with a spatula.
   - If using, sprinkle the streusel topping evenly over the batter.
   - Bake in the preheated oven for 35-40 minutes, or until a toothpick inserted into the center of the cake comes out clean. The cake should be golden brown and firm to the touch.

4. **Prepare the Glaze (if using):**
   - In a small bowl, whisk together the powdered sugar, orange juice, and vanilla extract until smooth. Adjust the consistency with more powdered sugar or orange juice if needed.

5. **Cool and Serve:**
   - Allow the cake to cool in the pan for 10 minutes before transferring to a wire rack to cool completely.
   - Once cooled, drizzle with the orange glaze if desired.

6. **Serving:**
   - Serve the cake plain, or with a dusting of powdered sugar, a dollop of whipped cream, or alongside a cup of tea or coffee.

Tips

- **Cranberries:** If using fresh cranberries, make sure they are washed and sorted. Frozen cranberries should be thawed and drained well to avoid excess moisture in the cake.
- **Walnuts:** Toasting the walnuts before adding them enhances their flavor. Simply place them in a dry skillet over medium heat and cook until fragrant, about 5 minutes, stirring occasionally.
- **Glaze:** The glaze adds a nice touch of sweetness and a hint of orange flavor. It can be omitted if you prefer a less sweet cake.

Cranberry Walnut Cake is a perfect blend of sweet and tart flavors, with a moist crumb and crunchy texture from the walnuts. This cake is a wonderful way to celebrate the flavors of the season and makes a memorable dessert for any special occasion.

Maple Walnut Brownies

Ingredients

For the Brownies:

- **1/2 cup (1 stick) unsalted butter**
- **1 cup granulated sugar**
- **1/4 cup pure maple syrup**
- **2 large eggs**
- **1 teaspoon vanilla extract**
- **1/2 cup unsweetened cocoa powder**
- **1/2 cup all-purpose flour**
- **1/4 teaspoon salt**
- **1/4 teaspoon baking powder**
- **1/2 cup chopped walnuts** (toasted if desired)

For the Maple Glaze (Optional):

- **1/2 cup powdered sugar**
- **2 tablespoons pure maple syrup**
- **1 tablespoon milk** (or more as needed for consistency)

Instructions

1. **Prepare the Brownie Batter:**
    - Preheat your oven to 350°F (175°C). Grease and flour an 8x8-inch baking pan or line it with parchment paper.
    - In a medium saucepan, melt the butter over low heat. Remove from heat and stir in the granulated sugar and maple syrup until well combined.
    - Allow the mixture to cool slightly, then whisk in the eggs and vanilla extract until smooth.
    - Sift in the cocoa powder, flour, salt, and baking powder. Stir until just combined, being careful not to overmix.
    - Fold in the chopped walnuts.
2. **Bake the Brownies:**
    - Pour the brownie batter into the prepared baking pan and spread it evenly with a spatula.
    - Bake in the preheated oven for 25-30 minutes, or until a toothpick inserted into the center comes out with just a few moist crumbs. The edges should be set and the center should still be slightly soft.
    - Allow the brownies to cool in the pan on a wire rack before cutting into squares.
3. **Prepare the Maple Glaze (Optional):**

- In a small bowl, whisk together the powdered sugar, maple syrup, and milk until smooth. Adjust the consistency with more milk or powdered sugar if needed.
- Drizzle the glaze over the cooled brownies for added sweetness and a glossy finish.

4. **Serve:**
   - Cut the brownies into squares and serve. They can be enjoyed as-is, or with a scoop of vanilla ice cream for an extra special treat.

Tips

- **Toasting Walnuts:** To toast walnuts, place them in a dry skillet over medium heat, stirring frequently until they are fragrant and slightly browned. This enhances their flavor and adds extra crunch.
- **Maple Syrup:** Use pure maple syrup for the best flavor. Imitation maple syrup can be used in a pinch but may not provide the same depth of taste.
- **Fudgy Brownies:** For extra fudginess, be careful not to overbake the brownies. They should still be a bit soft in the center when you take them out of the oven.

Maple Walnut Brownies offer a wonderful combination of chocolate and maple flavors with a satisfying nutty crunch. They are a perfect fall treat or an elegant twist on classic brownies, sure to be a hit with anyone who loves rich, flavorful desserts.

Mocha Maple Mousse

Ingredients

For the Mousse:

- 1 cup heavy cream
- 1/2 cup whole milk
- 1/4 cup pure maple syrup
- 1/4 cup brewed espresso (or strong coffee, cooled)
- 4 ounces semi-sweet chocolate (chopped)
- 1/2 teaspoon instant coffee granules (optional, for extra coffee flavor)
- 1 teaspoon vanilla extract
- 2 large egg yolks

For Garnish (Optional):

- Whipped cream
- Chocolate shavings
- Maple syrup drizzle
- Coffee beans or cocoa powder

Instructions

1. **Prepare the Chocolate Mixture:**
   - In a small saucepan, combine the milk, maple syrup, and espresso. Heat over medium heat until the mixture is hot but not boiling.
   - Remove from heat and add the chopped semi-sweet chocolate. Stir until the chocolate is completely melted and smooth. If using, stir in the instant coffee granules for a stronger coffee flavor. Set aside to cool slightly.
2. **Prepare the Egg Yolks:**
   - In a separate bowl, whisk the egg yolks lightly.
   - Gradually add a small amount of the hot milk mixture to the egg yolks, whisking constantly to temper the eggs and prevent curdling.
   - Return the egg yolk mixture to the saucepan with the remaining milk mixture. Cook over medium heat, stirring constantly, until the mixture thickens slightly and coats the back of a spoon. Do not let it boil.
3. **Combine and Chill:**
   - Remove the saucepan from heat and stir in the vanilla extract.
   - Allow the mixture to cool to room temperature, stirring occasionally.
4. **Whip the Cream:**
   - In a large bowl, whip the heavy cream until stiff peaks form. Be careful not to overwhip.

5. **Fold the Mixtures Together:**
   - Gently fold the cooled chocolate mixture into the whipped cream, being careful not to deflate the cream. Fold until well combined and smooth.
6. **Chill the Mousse:**
   - Spoon the mousse into individual serving dishes or glasses. Refrigerate for at least 2 hours, or until set.
7. **Garnish and Serve:**
   - Before serving, garnish with a dollop of whipped cream, chocolate shavings, a drizzle of maple syrup, and/or a few coffee beans or a sprinkle of cocoa powder if desired.

Tips

- **Chocolate:** Use high-quality semi-sweet chocolate for the best flavor and texture. You can also use dark chocolate if you prefer a richer taste.
- **Coffee:** Adjust the amount of espresso or coffee according to your taste preference. For a stronger coffee flavor, increase the amount of instant coffee granules.
- **Make Ahead:** The mousse can be made up to 2 days in advance and stored in the refrigerator. Just add the garnish before serving.

Mocha Maple Mousse offers a sophisticated blend of flavors with a creamy, airy texture that's perfect for a special dessert. The combination of coffee, chocolate, and maple creates a rich and indulgent treat that will impress your guests and satisfy your sweet tooth.

Maple Glazed Cheesecake

Ingredients

For the Crust:

- 1 1/2 cups graham cracker crumbs
- 1/4 cup granulated sugar
- 1/2 cup unsalted butter (melted)

For the Cheesecake Filling:

- 4 (8-ounce) packages cream cheese (softened)
- 1 cup granulated sugar
- 1 cup sour cream
- 1 cup heavy cream
- 4 large eggs
- 2 teaspoons vanilla extract
- 1 tablespoon all-purpose flour

For the Maple Glaze:

- 1/2 cup pure maple syrup
- 2 tablespoons unsalted butter
- 1/4 cup heavy cream
- 1 tablespoon cornstarch
- 1 tablespoon water

Instructions

1. **Prepare the Crust:**
    - Preheat your oven to 325°F (163°C). Grease the sides of a 9-inch springform pan or line it with parchment paper.
    - In a medium bowl, combine the graham cracker crumbs, granulated sugar, and melted butter. Mix until the crumbs are evenly coated with butter.
    - Press the crumb mixture firmly into the bottom of the prepared pan to form an even layer. Bake for 10 minutes, then remove from the oven and let cool.
2. **Prepare the Cheesecake Filling:**
    - In a large mixing bowl, beat the cream cheese until smooth and creamy. Gradually add the granulated sugar, beating until fully combined.
    - Add the sour cream and heavy cream, and continue to beat until smooth.
    - Mix in the eggs one at a time, beating well after each addition. Add the vanilla extract and flour, mixing until just combined.

- Pour the cheesecake filling over the cooled crust in the springform pan.
3. **Bake the Cheesecake:**
    - Bake the cheesecake in the preheated oven for 60-70 minutes, or until the center is set and the edges are lightly golden. The center may still be slightly jiggly; it will firm up as it cools.
    - Turn off the oven and let the cheesecake cool in the oven with the door slightly ajar for 1 hour. Then, remove the cheesecake from the oven and let it cool to room temperature before refrigerating. Chill in the refrigerator for at least 4 hours or overnight.
4. **Prepare the Maple Glaze:**
    - In a small saucepan, combine the maple syrup and butter. Heat over medium heat until the butter is melted and the mixture is well combined.
    - In a small bowl, mix the cornstarch with water to form a slurry. Add this mixture to the saucepan and stir continuously until the glaze thickens, about 2-3 minutes.
    - Remove from heat and let the glaze cool to room temperature.
5. **Assemble and Serve:**
    - Once the cheesecake has chilled and set, remove it from the springform pan.
    - Pour the cooled maple glaze evenly over the top of the cheesecake, spreading it gently with a spatula to cover the surface.
    - Return the cheesecake to the refrigerator for an additional 30 minutes to allow the glaze to set.
6. **Garnish (Optional):**
    - Garnish with a drizzle of additional maple syrup, a sprinkle of chopped nuts, or a few fresh berries for added texture and flavor.

Tips

- **Cheese:** Ensure the cream cheese is fully softened to prevent lumps in the filling.
- **Crust:** Press the crust mixture firmly into the pan to ensure it holds together well after baking.
- **Glaze:** The maple glaze can be made a day ahead and stored in the refrigerator. Reheat slightly before using if it thickens too much.

Maple Glazed Cheesecake is a delightful fusion of classic cheesecake with a touch of maple sweetness. The creamy, rich texture of the cheesecake paired with the glossy, flavorful maple glaze makes for a stunning and delicious dessert that's sure to impress.

Pumpkin Chiffon Pie

Ingredients

For the Crust:

- 1 1/2 cups graham cracker crumbs
- 1/4 cup granulated sugar
- 1/4 cup unsalted butter (melted)

For the Chiffon Filling:

- 1 cup canned pumpkin puree (not pumpkin pie filling)
- 1/2 cup granulated sugar
- 1/2 teaspoon ground cinnamon
- 1/4 teaspoon ground ginger
- 1/4 teaspoon ground nutmeg
- 1/4 teaspoon salt
- 1/4 cup water
- 1 tablespoon unflavored gelatin
- 3 large egg yolks
- 1/2 cup whole milk
- 1 teaspoon vanilla extract
- 3 large egg whites
- 1/4 teaspoon cream of tartar
- 1/4 cup granulated sugar (for egg whites)

For the Whipped Cream Topping:

- 1 cup heavy cream
- 2 tablespoons powdered sugar
- 1 teaspoon vanilla extract

Instructions

1. **Prepare the Crust:**
   - Preheat your oven to 350°F (175°C). Grease a 9-inch pie dish or line it with parchment paper.
   - In a medium bowl, combine the graham cracker crumbs, granulated sugar, and melted butter. Mix until the crumbs are evenly coated with butter.
   - Press the crumb mixture firmly into the bottom and up the sides of the prepared pie dish to form an even layer.
   - Bake for 10 minutes, then remove from the oven and let cool completely.

2. **Prepare the Chiffon Filling:**
    - In a small saucepan, combine the water and gelatin. Let it sit for about 5 minutes to bloom the gelatin.
    - Heat the gelatin mixture over low heat until the gelatin is completely dissolved. Remove from heat and set aside.
    - In a large bowl, whisk together the pumpkin puree, granulated sugar, cinnamon, ginger, nutmeg, and salt.
    - In a separate saucepan, whisk the egg yolks and milk together, then cook over medium heat, stirring constantly until the mixture thickens slightly (about 5 minutes). Do not let it boil.
    - Remove the custard mixture from heat and stir in the dissolved gelatin and vanilla extract. Allow to cool slightly.
    - In a large mixing bowl, beat the egg whites and cream of tartar until soft peaks form. Gradually add the 1/4 cup granulated sugar, continuing to beat until stiff peaks form.
    - Gently fold the egg whites into the pumpkin mixture until fully incorporated.
3. **Assemble the Pie:**
    - Pour the pumpkin chiffon filling into the cooled graham cracker crust, spreading it evenly with a spatula.
    - Refrigerate for at least 4 hours or until the filling is fully set.
4. **Prepare the Whipped Cream Topping:**
    - In a chilled mixing bowl, whip the heavy cream with the powdered sugar and vanilla extract until stiff peaks form.
    - Spread the whipped cream over the chilled pumpkin chiffon pie.
5. **Serve:**
    - Garnish the pie with a sprinkle of ground cinnamon or nutmeg, if desired.
    - Slice and serve chilled. The pie can be stored in the refrigerator for up to 3 days.

Tips

- **Gelatin:** Ensure the gelatin is fully dissolved before adding it to the pumpkin mixture to avoid lumps.
- **Egg Whites:** For best results, make sure the mixing bowl and beaters are clean and free from any grease when whipping the egg whites.
- **Crust:** If you prefer, you can use a pre-made pie crust instead of making the graham cracker crust.

Pumpkin Chiffon Pie is a delightful and elegant dessert that offers a lighter take on traditional pumpkin pie. The airy, creamy filling paired with a crisp graham cracker crust and topped with whipped cream makes for a truly irresistible treat that's perfect for any fall or holiday occasion.

Apple Cinnamon Roll Casserole

Ingredients

For the Casserole:

- **2 cans (12.4 ounces each) refrigerated cinnamon rolls** (with icing)
- **2 cups diced apples** (peeled and cored)
- **1 tablespoon lemon juice**
- **1/4 cup granulated sugar**
- **1 teaspoon ground cinnamon**
- **1/2 teaspoon ground nutmeg**
- **1/2 cup chopped pecans** (optional)
- **1/2 cup milk**
- **3 large eggs**

For the Glaze:

- **1/2 cup powdered sugar**
- **2 tablespoons milk**
- **1/2 teaspoon vanilla extract**

Instructions

1. **Prepare the Apples:**
   - Preheat your oven to 350°F (175°C).
   - In a medium bowl, toss the diced apples with lemon juice, granulated sugar, ground cinnamon, and ground nutmeg. Set aside.
2. **Prepare the Cinnamon Rolls:**
   - Open the cans of cinnamon rolls and cut each roll into quarters. Place the pieces in a large bowl.
   - Gently fold in the spiced apple mixture and chopped pecans (if using).
3. **Assemble the Casserole:**
   - Grease a 9x13-inch baking dish or spray it with non-stick cooking spray.
   - Arrange the cinnamon roll and apple mixture evenly in the prepared baking dish.
   - In a separate bowl, whisk together the milk and eggs. Pour this mixture evenly over the cinnamon roll and apple mixture in the baking dish.
4. **Bake the Casserole:**
   - Bake in the preheated oven for 35-40 minutes, or until the casserole is golden brown and a knife inserted into the center comes out clean. The top should be set and slightly crisped.
5. **Prepare the Glaze:**

- While the casserole is baking, prepare the glaze. In a small bowl, whisk together the powdered sugar, milk, and vanilla extract until smooth.
6. **Finish and Serve:**
    - Allow the casserole to cool slightly before drizzling the glaze over the top.
    - Serve warm, straight from the dish. It's great on its own or with a side of fresh fruit.

Tips

- **Apples:** Choose firm apples like Honeycrisp or Granny Smith for the best texture and flavor. They hold up well during baking and add a nice contrast to the sweetness of the cinnamon rolls.
- **Cinnamon Rolls:** You can use any flavor of refrigerated cinnamon rolls, but the classic cinnamon roll flavor pairs best with the apple filling.
- **Make-Ahead:** You can prepare the casserole up to a day in advance. Assemble the casserole, cover it with plastic wrap or aluminum foil, and refrigerate overnight. Bake the next morning, adding a few extra minutes to the baking time if needed.

Apple Cinnamon Roll Casserole combines the comforting flavors of cinnamon rolls with the fresh, fruity taste of apples, all topped with a sweet glaze. It's an indulgent yet easy dish that's perfect for special occasions or a cozy breakfast at home.

Chocolate Maple Torte

Ingredients

For the Chocolate Cake:

- 1 cup (6 ounces) semi-sweet chocolate chips (or chopped chocolate)
- 1/2 cup unsalted butter
- 1 cup granulated sugar
- 3 large eggs
- 1 teaspoon vanilla extract
- 1/2 cup all-purpose flour
- 1/4 teaspoon salt
- 1/4 teaspoon baking powder

For the Maple Cream Filling:

- 1 cup heavy cream
- 1/4 cup pure maple syrup
- 1 teaspoon vanilla extract
- 2 tablespoons powdered sugar

For the Maple Glaze:

- 1/2 cup pure maple syrup
- 2 tablespoons unsalted butter
- 1/4 cup heavy cream
- 1 tablespoon cornstarch
- 1 tablespoon water

Instructions

1. **Prepare the Chocolate Cake:**
    - Preheat your oven to 350°F (175°C). Grease and flour an 8-inch round cake pan or line it with parchment paper.
    - In a medium saucepan, melt the chocolate chips and butter over low heat, stirring until smooth. Remove from heat and let cool slightly.
    - Stir in the granulated sugar until well combined.
    - Beat in the eggs one at a time, mixing well after each addition. Add the vanilla extract.
    - Sift together the flour, salt, and baking powder, then fold them into the chocolate mixture until just combined.
    - Pour the batter into the prepared cake pan and smooth the top.

- Bake for 25-30 minutes, or until a toothpick inserted into the center comes out clean. Let the cake cool in the pan for 10 minutes, then turn it out onto a wire rack to cool completely.
2. **Prepare the Maple Cream Filling:**
    - In a medium mixing bowl, beat the heavy cream with an electric mixer until soft peaks form.
    - Gradually add the powdered sugar and vanilla extract, and continue beating until stiff peaks form.
    - Gently fold in the maple syrup until well incorporated.
3. **Prepare the Maple Glaze:**
    - In a small saucepan, combine the maple syrup and butter. Heat over medium heat until the butter is melted and the mixture is well combined.
    - In a small bowl, mix the cornstarch with water to form a slurry. Add this mixture to the saucepan and stir continuously until the glaze thickens, about 2-3 minutes. Remove from heat and let cool slightly.
4. **Assemble the Torte:**
    - Once the chocolate cake has cooled, carefully slice it in half horizontally to create two layers.
    - Place one layer on a serving plate or cake stand. Spread the maple cream filling evenly over the top.
    - Place the second layer of cake on top of the filling.
    - Pour the maple glaze over the top of the torte, allowing it to drizzle down the sides.
5. **Serve:**
    - Allow the torte to set for about 30 minutes before slicing to let the glaze firm up slightly.
    - Garnish with additional maple syrup drizzle or chocolate shavings, if desired.

Tips

- **Chocolate:** Use high-quality semi-sweet chocolate for the best flavor and texture. You can also use bittersweet chocolate for a richer taste.
- **Maple Syrup:** Use pure maple syrup for the best flavor. Imitation maple syrup may not provide the same depth of taste.
- **Chilling:** For a firmer texture, refrigerate the torte for about an hour before serving.

Chocolate Maple Torte is a luxurious dessert that beautifully marries the richness of chocolate with the sweetness of maple syrup. With its layers of creamy filling and glossy glaze, it's an impressive and delectable choice for any special occasion.

Raspberry Lemon Bars

Ingredients

For the Crust:

- **1 1/2 cups all-purpose flour**
- **1/2 cup granulated sugar**
- **1/2 teaspoon baking powder**
- **1/4 teaspoon salt**
- **1/2 cup unsalted butter** (cold and cut into small pieces)

For the Raspberry Layer:

- **1 cup fresh raspberries** (or frozen, thawed)
- **1/4 cup granulated sugar**
- **1 tablespoon lemon juice**

For the Lemon Filling:

- **4 large eggs**
- **1 1/2 cups granulated sugar**
- **1/2 cup freshly squeezed lemon juice** (about 2-3 lemons)
- **1/4 cup all-purpose flour**
- **1/2 teaspoon baking powder**
- **1/4 teaspoon salt**

For Garnish (Optional):

- **Powdered sugar** (for dusting)
- **Fresh raspberries** (for decoration)
- **Lemon zest**

Instructions

1. **Prepare the Crust:**
    - Preheat your oven to 350°F (175°C). Grease and line an 8x8-inch baking pan with parchment paper, leaving a bit of an overhang for easy removal.
    - In a medium bowl, whisk together the flour, granulated sugar, baking powder, and salt.
    - Cut in the cold butter using a pastry cutter or your fingers until the mixture resembles coarse crumbs.
    - Press the mixture evenly into the bottom of the prepared baking pan.

- Bake for 15-20 minutes, or until the crust is lightly golden. Remove from the oven and set aside.
2. **Prepare the Raspberry Layer:**
   - In a small saucepan, combine the raspberries, granulated sugar, and lemon juice. Cook over medium heat, stirring occasionally, until the raspberries break down and the mixture thickens slightly (about 5 minutes).
   - Let the raspberry mixture cool, then strain it through a fine mesh sieve to remove seeds, if desired. Set aside.
3. **Prepare the Lemon Filling:**
   - In a large mixing bowl, whisk the eggs until well beaten. Add the granulated sugar and lemon juice, and whisk until combined.
   - Sift in the flour, baking powder, and salt. Stir until smooth and fully combined.
4. **Assemble the Bars:**
   - Pour the lemon filling over the partially baked crust, spreading it evenly.
   - Drop spoonfuls of the raspberry puree over the lemon filling. Use a toothpick or a skewer to gently swirl the raspberry puree into the lemon filling, creating a marbled effect.
5. **Bake the Bars:**
   - Bake in the preheated oven for 25-30 minutes, or until the lemon filling is set and the edges are lightly golden. A toothpick inserted into the center should come out clean.
   - Allow the bars to cool completely in the pan on a wire rack before slicing.
6. **Garnish and Serve:**
   - Once cooled, dust the top with powdered sugar, if desired. Garnish with fresh raspberries and lemon zest for a decorative touch.
   - Cut into squares and serve.

Tips

- **Raspberries:** Fresh raspberries are best, but if using frozen, be sure to thaw and drain them well before cooking to avoid excess moisture.
- **Lemon Juice:** Freshly squeezed lemon juice provides the best flavor. Avoid using bottled lemon juice if possible.
- **Cooling:** Allow the bars to cool completely before cutting to ensure clean slices and proper setting of the filling.

Raspberry Lemon Bars offer a delightful combination of tangy lemon and sweet raspberry flavors in every bite. With their vibrant colors and refreshing taste, they make for an irresistible and elegant dessert that's sure to impress.

Maple Butter Cake

Ingredients

For the Cake:

- 1 cup unsalted butter (softened)
- 1 cup granulated sugar
- 1/2 cup packed brown sugar
- 4 large eggs
- 1 cup pure maple syrup
- 1/2 cup milk
- 2 1/2 cups all-purpose flour
- 2 teaspoons baking powder
- 1/2 teaspoon salt
- 1 teaspoon vanilla extract

For the Maple Glaze:

- 1/2 cup pure maple syrup
- 1/4 cup unsalted butter
- 1 cup powdered sugar
- 1/4 teaspoon vanilla extract

Instructions

1. **Prepare the Cake:**
    - Preheat your oven to 350°F (175°C). Grease and flour a 9x13-inch baking pan or two 8-inch round cake pans. Line the bottom of the pans with parchment paper for easy removal.
    - In a large mixing bowl, cream together the softened butter, granulated sugar, and brown sugar until light and fluffy.
    - Beat in the eggs one at a time, making sure each egg is fully incorporated before adding the next.
    - Mix in the maple syrup and vanilla extract.
    - In a separate bowl, whisk together the flour, baking powder, and salt.
    - Gradually add the dry ingredients to the wet ingredients, alternating with the milk, beginning and ending with the dry ingredients. Mix until just combined.
    - Pour the batter into the prepared pan(s) and smooth the top with a spatula.
    - Bake for 30-35 minutes (for the 9x13 pan) or 25-30 minutes (for the round pans), or until a toothpick inserted into the center of the cake comes out clean. The cake should be golden brown and spring back when lightly touched.

- Allow the cake to cool in the pan for 10 minutes, then transfer to a wire rack to cool completely.
2. **Prepare the Maple Glaze:**
    - In a small saucepan, combine the maple syrup and butter. Heat over medium heat until the butter is melted and the mixture is well combined.
    - Remove from heat and whisk in the powdered sugar and vanilla extract until smooth. If the glaze is too thick, add a little more maple syrup or milk to reach your desired consistency.
3. **Glaze the Cake:**
    - Once the cake has cooled completely, pour the maple glaze over the top, allowing it to drip down the sides. Use a spatula to spread the glaze evenly if needed.
4. **Serve:**
    - Let the glaze set for about 30 minutes before slicing the cake.
    - Cut into squares or slices and serve. The cake can be stored in an airtight container at room temperature for up to 3 days, or in the refrigerator for up to a week.

Tips

- **Maple Syrup:** Use high-quality pure maple syrup for the best flavor. Avoid imitation maple syrup, which can have a less authentic taste.
- **Butter:** Make sure the butter is softened to room temperature to ensure it blends well with the sugar.
- **Glaze Consistency:** Adjust the thickness of the glaze by adding more powdered sugar if you prefer a thicker glaze or more syrup if you want it thinner.

Maple Butter Cake is a delectable dessert that showcases the rich, warm flavors of maple syrup in a moist, buttery cake. Topped with a sweet maple glaze, it's a treat that's sure to delight anyone who loves the comforting taste of maple.

Cinnamon Sugar Beignets

Ingredients

For the Beignet Dough:

- **1 cup whole milk**
- **1/4 cup granulated sugar**
- **2 1/4 teaspoons active dry yeast** (1 packet)
- **1/4 cup unsalted butter** (softened)
- **1 large egg**
- **1/2 teaspoon vanilla extract**
- **3 1/2 cups all-purpose flour** (plus extra for dusting)
- **1/2 teaspoon salt**
- **Vegetable oil** (for frying)

For the Cinnamon Sugar Coating:

- **1 cup granulated sugar**
- **1 tablespoon ground cinnamon**

Instructions

1. **Prepare the Dough:**
   - In a small saucepan, warm the milk over low heat until it reaches about 110°F (43°C). Remove from heat and sprinkle the yeast over the milk. Let it sit for 5 minutes, or until the mixture is frothy.
   - In a large mixing bowl, combine the sugar, softened butter, egg, and vanilla extract. Mix until well combined.
   - Add the yeast mixture to the bowl and stir to combine.
   - Gradually add the flour and salt, mixing until a soft dough forms. You may need to add a bit more flour if the dough is too sticky.
   - Turn the dough out onto a floured surface and knead for about 5-7 minutes, or until it is smooth and elastic.
   - Place the dough in a lightly greased bowl, cover with a clean kitchen towel, and let it rise in a warm place for 1-2 hours, or until doubled in size.
2. **Roll and Cut the Dough:**
   - Once the dough has risen, punch it down and turn it out onto a floured surface. Roll it out to about 1/4-inch thickness.
   - Using a knife or a pizza cutter, cut the dough into 2-inch squares.
3. **Heat the Oil:**

- In a large, heavy-bottomed pot or deep fryer, heat about 2 inches of vegetable oil to 350°F (175°C). Use a thermometer to ensure the oil is at the correct temperature.
4. **Fry the Beignets:**
    - Carefully drop a few dough squares into the hot oil at a time, being careful not to overcrowd the pot.
    - Fry the beignets for about 1-2 minutes per side, or until they are golden brown and puffed up.
    - Use a slotted spoon to transfer the beignets to a paper towel-lined plate to drain.
5. **Coat with Cinnamon Sugar:**
    - In a shallow dish, combine the granulated sugar and ground cinnamon.
    - While the beignets are still warm, toss them in the cinnamon sugar mixture until they are evenly coated.
6. **Serve:**
    - Serve the beignets warm, ideally right after they have been coated. They are best enjoyed fresh and can be accompanied by a cup of coffee or hot chocolate.

Tips

- **Dough Rising:** Ensure the dough is placed in a warm, draft-free area for optimal rising. You can use an oven with the light on or a warm corner of your kitchen.
- **Oil Temperature:** Maintain a consistent oil temperature to avoid overcooking or undercooking the beignets. If the oil is too hot, the beignets may cook too quickly on the outside while remaining raw inside.
- **Flour:** If the dough is too sticky to handle, add a little more flour as needed. Just be careful not to add too much, or the beignets may become dense.

Cinnamon Sugar Beignets are a delightful treat that combines the soft, pillowy texture of classic beignets with the warm, sweet flavors of cinnamon and sugar. These indulgent pastries are perfect for any occasion and are sure to be a hit with family and friends.

Blueberry Lemon Cheesecake Bars

Ingredients

For the Crust:

- **1 1/2 cups graham cracker crumbs** (about 10-12 graham crackers)
- **1/4 cup granulated sugar**
- **1/2 cup unsalted butter** (melted)

For the Cheesecake Filling:

- **16 ounces cream cheese** (softened)
- **1/2 cup granulated sugar**
- **1/4 cup sour cream**
- **2 large eggs**
- **1/4 cup freshly squeezed lemon juice**
- **1 teaspoon lemon zest**
- **1 teaspoon vanilla extract**

For the Blueberry Swirl:

- **1 cup fresh or frozen blueberries**
- **1/4 cup granulated sugar**
- **1 tablespoon lemon juice**
- **1 teaspoon cornstarch**
- **1 tablespoon water**

Instructions

1. **Prepare the Crust:**
    - Preheat your oven to 325°F (160°C). Grease and line an 8x8-inch baking pan with parchment paper, leaving an overhang for easy removal.
    - In a medium bowl, combine the graham cracker crumbs, granulated sugar, and melted butter. Stir until the mixture resembles wet sand.
    - Press the crumb mixture evenly into the bottom of the prepared pan to form the crust. Use the back of a spoon to compact it.
    - Bake the crust in the preheated oven for 8-10 minutes, or until lightly golden. Remove from the oven and let it cool slightly.
2. **Prepare the Blueberry Swirl:**
    - In a small saucepan, combine the blueberries, granulated sugar, lemon juice, cornstarch, and water. Cook over medium heat, stirring frequently, until the blueberries burst and the mixture thickens, about 5-7 minutes.

- Remove from heat and let the blueberry mixture cool slightly.
3. **Prepare the Cheesecake Filling:**
    - In a large mixing bowl, beat the softened cream cheese until smooth and creamy.
    - Add the granulated sugar and sour cream, and beat until well combined.
    - Beat in the eggs one at a time, mixing well after each addition.
    - Add the lemon juice, lemon zest, and vanilla extract, and mix until smooth.
4. **Assemble the Bars:**
    - Pour the cheesecake filling over the pre-baked crust, spreading it evenly with a spatula.
    - Drop spoonfuls of the blueberry mixture over the cheesecake filling. Use a knife or a toothpick to gently swirl the blueberry mixture into the cheesecake, creating a marbled effect.
5. **Bake the Bars:**
    - Bake in the preheated oven for 35-40 minutes, or until the cheesecake is set and the edges are lightly golden. The center should still be slightly jiggly but firm.
    - Turn off the oven and crack the oven door slightly. Let the cheesecake cool in the oven for 1 hour. This helps prevent cracking.
6. **Chill and Serve:**
    - After cooling, refrigerate the cheesecake bars for at least 3 hours, or overnight, to allow them to fully set.
    - Once chilled, lift the bars out of the pan using the parchment paper overhang and cut into squares.
7. **Garnish (Optional):**
    - Garnish with fresh blueberries and a sprinkle of lemon zest before serving, if desired.

Tips

- **Cream Cheese:** Make sure the cream cheese is softened to room temperature for a smooth filling. Cold cream cheese can result in lumps.
- **Blueberries:** If using frozen blueberries, thaw them and drain excess liquid before cooking to avoid a watery swirl.
- **Swirling:** Don't over-swirl the blueberry mixture into the cheesecake. A few gentle swirls will create a beautiful marbled effect without blending the layers too much.

Blueberry Lemon Cheesecake Bars offer a delightful blend of tangy lemon and sweet blueberries in every bite. With their creamy texture and vibrant flavor, these bars are sure to be a hit at any gathering or simply enjoyed as a special treat.

Maple Walnut Fudge

Ingredients

- **1 cup pure maple syrup**
- **1 cup granulated sugar**
- **1/2 cup unsalted butter** (cut into small pieces)
- **1/2 cup heavy cream**
- **1/4 teaspoon salt**
- **1/2 teaspoon vanilla extract**
- **1 cup chopped walnuts** (toasted)

Instructions

1. **Prepare the Pan:**
    - Line an 8x8-inch baking pan with parchment paper, leaving an overhang for easy removal. Grease the parchment paper lightly or use a non-stick spray.
2. **Cook the Fudge Mixture:**
    - In a medium saucepan, combine the maple syrup, granulated sugar, butter, heavy cream, and salt.
    - Place the saucepan over medium heat and cook, stirring constantly, until the mixture comes to a boil.
    - Continue to cook the mixture, stirring frequently, until it reaches the soft-ball stage (about 234°F to 240°F or 112°C to 115°C) on a candy thermometer. This should take about 10-12 minutes. Be cautious not to overcook, as this can affect the texture of the fudge.
3. **Add Flavor and Nuts:**
    - Remove the saucepan from heat and stir in the vanilla extract.
    - Allow the mixture to cool slightly for about 5 minutes.
    - Gently fold in the toasted walnuts.
4. **Pour and Set:**
    - Pour the fudge mixture into the prepared baking pan and spread it evenly with a spatula.
    - Let the fudge cool at room temperature for about 2-3 hours, or until it is set and firm.
5. **Cut and Serve:**
    - Once the fudge is fully set, lift it out of the pan using the parchment paper overhang.
    - Cut into squares or desired shapes.
6. **Store:**
    - Store the fudge in an airtight container at room temperature for up to 2 weeks. For longer storage, you can refrigerate it for up to a month.

Tips

- **Maple Syrup:** Use pure maple syrup for the best flavor. Imitation maple syrup will not provide the same depth of taste.
- **Candy Thermometer:** For best results, use a candy thermometer to ensure the fudge reaches the correct temperature. This ensures a smooth texture.
- **Toasting Walnuts:** Toast the walnuts in a dry skillet over medium heat for a few minutes until fragrant. This enhances their flavor and crunchiness.

Maple Walnut Fudge is a delightful treat that combines the rich, sweet taste of maple with the crunchy texture of walnuts. With its creamy texture and delicious flavor, it's a perfect addition to any dessert table or as a homemade gift for loved ones.

Sour Cherry Pie

Ingredients

For the Pie Crust:

- **2 1/2 cups all-purpose flour**
- **1 cup unsalted butter** (cold and cut into small pieces)
- **1/4 cup granulated sugar**
- **1/2 teaspoon salt**
- **1/4 to 1/2 cup ice water**

For the Cherry Filling:

- **4 cups sour cherries** (pitted; fresh or frozen, thawed and drained)
- **1 cup granulated sugar**
- **1/4 cup cornstarch**
- **1/4 teaspoon salt**
- **1/4 teaspoon almond extract**
- **1 tablespoon lemon juice**
- **1/4 teaspoon ground cinnamon** (optional)

For Assembly:

- **1 tablespoon unsalted butter** (cut into small pieces)
- **1 egg** (beaten, for egg wash)
- **1 tablespoon granulated sugar** (for sprinkling)

Instructions

1. **Prepare the Pie Crust:**
    - In a large bowl, whisk together the flour, granulated sugar, and salt.
    - Add the cold butter pieces and use a pastry cutter or your fingers to work the butter into the flour mixture until it resembles coarse crumbs.
    - Gradually add ice water, 1 tablespoon at a time, mixing until the dough just begins to come together. You may not need all the water.
    - Divide the dough in half, form each half into a disk, and wrap in plastic wrap. Chill in the refrigerator for at least 1 hour.
2. **Prepare the Cherry Filling:**
    - In a large bowl, combine the pitted cherries, granulated sugar, cornstarch, salt, almond extract, lemon juice, and cinnamon (if using). Stir until the cherries are evenly coated and the mixture is well combined.
3. **Assemble the Pie:**

- Preheat your oven to 425°F (220°C).
- On a lightly floured surface, roll out one disk of dough to fit a 9-inch pie dish. Carefully transfer the rolled dough to the pie dish and press it into the bottom and sides.
- Pour the cherry filling into the prepared crust, and dot the filling with small pieces of butter.
- Roll out the second disk of dough and place it over the cherry filling. Trim any excess dough and crimp the edges to seal. You can also create a lattice top if desired.
- Brush the top crust with the beaten egg and sprinkle with granulated sugar for a nice shine and a touch of sweetness.

4. **Bake the Pie:**
   - Place the pie on a baking sheet to catch any drips. Bake in the preheated oven for 45-55 minutes, or until the crust is golden brown and the filling is bubbling.
   - If the edges of the crust start to brown too quickly, cover them with aluminum foil to prevent burning.

5. **Cool and Serve:**
   - Allow the pie to cool completely on a wire rack before slicing. This helps the filling to set and makes for cleaner slices.

6. **Store:**
   - Store leftover pie at room temperature for up to 2 days, or refrigerate for up to 5 days. The pie can also be frozen for up to 3 months. To reheat, bake in a preheated oven at 350°F (175°C) until warmed through.

Tips

- **Sour Cherries:** If using frozen cherries, ensure they are well-drained to avoid a watery filling.
- **Crust:** For an extra flaky crust, use chilled utensils and work the dough quickly to keep the butter from melting.
- **Thickening:** The cornstarch in the filling helps to thicken the juice and keep the filling from being runny.

Sour Cherry Pie offers a delightful balance of tart cherries and sweet, buttery crust. Its vibrant flavor and beautiful appearance make it a standout dessert for any occasion.

Vanilla Bean Ice Cream with Maple Syrup

Ingredients

For the Vanilla Bean Ice Cream:

- **2 cups heavy cream**
- **1 cup whole milk**
- **3/4 cup granulated sugar**
- **1 vanilla bean** (split and scraped, or 1 tablespoon vanilla extract)
- **4 large egg yolks**

For the Maple Syrup Sauce:

- **1/2 cup pure maple syrup**
- **1/4 cup heavy cream**

Instructions

1. **Prepare the Vanilla Bean Ice Cream Base:**
    - In a medium saucepan, combine the heavy cream, whole milk, and granulated sugar. If using a vanilla bean, add both the seeds and the pod to the mixture.
    - Heat over medium heat until the mixture is steaming but not boiling. Remove from heat and let it steep for about 10 minutes to infuse the vanilla flavor.
    - In a separate bowl, whisk the egg yolks until pale and slightly thickened.
    - Gradually add a few spoonfuls of the hot cream mixture to the egg yolks, whisking constantly to temper them.
    - Slowly pour the tempered egg yolks back into the saucepan, whisking continuously.
    - Return the saucepan to the stove and cook over medium heat, stirring constantly, until the mixture thickens and coats the back of a spoon (about 170°F to 175°F or 77°C to 80°C). Do not let it boil.
    - Strain the mixture through a fine-mesh sieve into a clean bowl to remove any curdled bits and the vanilla bean pod.
2. **Chill the Custard:**
    - Cover the bowl with plastic wrap, pressing it directly onto the surface of the custard to prevent a skin from forming. Chill in the refrigerator for at least 4 hours or overnight until completely cold.
3. **Churn the Ice Cream:**
    - Pour the chilled custard into an ice cream maker and churn according to the manufacturer's instructions, usually for about 20-25 minutes, or until it reaches a soft-serve consistency.
4. **Prepare the Maple Syrup Sauce:**

- In a small saucepan, combine the maple syrup and heavy cream. Heat over medium heat, stirring frequently, until the mixture is warmed through and slightly thickened. Allow it to cool slightly.
5. **Serve:**
    - Transfer the churned ice cream to an airtight container and freeze for at least 2 hours to firm up.
    - Scoop the vanilla bean ice cream into bowls or cones and drizzle with the maple syrup sauce.

Tips

- **Vanilla Bean:** For a more intense vanilla flavor and attractive specks, use a vanilla bean. If using vanilla extract, add it after cooking the custard and before chilling.
- **Ice Cream Maker:** Ensure your ice cream maker's bowl is thoroughly chilled before churning for the best texture.
- **Maple Syrup:** Use high-quality pure maple syrup for the best flavor. Avoid imitation syrup for a richer taste.

Vanilla Bean Ice Cream with Maple Syrup offers a delightful blend of creamy vanilla and sweet, caramel-like maple. This sophisticated dessert is sure to impress and satisfy any ice cream lover.

Pumpkin Spice Cake

Ingredients

For the Cake:

- 1 1/2 cups all-purpose flour
- 1 teaspoon baking powder
- 1/2 teaspoon baking soda
- 1/2 teaspoon salt
- 1 teaspoon ground cinnamon
- 1/2 teaspoon ground ginger
- 1/4 teaspoon ground cloves
- 1/4 teaspoon ground nutmeg
- 1/2 cup unsalted butter (room temperature)
- 1 cup granulated sugar
- 1/2 cup packed light brown sugar
- 2 large eggs
- 1 cup canned pumpkin puree (not pumpkin pie filling)
- 1/2 cup sour cream
- 1/2 teaspoon vanilla extract

For the Cream Cheese Frosting (optional):

- 8 ounces cream cheese (softened)
- 1/2 cup unsalted butter (room temperature)
- 2 cups powdered sugar
- 1 teaspoon vanilla extract
- 1-2 tablespoons milk or heavy cream (if needed for consistency)

Instructions

1. **Prepare the Oven and Pans:**
   - Preheat your oven to 350°F (175°C).
   - Grease and flour a 9-inch round cake pan or line it with parchment paper. Alternatively, you can use two 8-inch round pans or a 9x13-inch baking dish.
2. **Mix Dry Ingredients:**
   - In a medium bowl, whisk together the flour, baking powder, baking soda, salt, cinnamon, ginger, cloves, and nutmeg. Set aside.
3. **Cream Butter and Sugars:**
   - In a large mixing bowl, use an electric mixer to beat the butter until creamy.
   - Add the granulated sugar and brown sugar, and continue to beat until light and fluffy.

4. **Add Eggs and Pumpkin:**
   - Add the eggs one at a time, beating well after each addition.
   - Mix in the pumpkin puree until well combined.
5. **Combine Dry and Wet Ingredients:**
   - Gradually add the dry ingredients to the butter mixture, alternating with the sour cream. Start and end with the dry ingredients. Mix until just combined; do not overmix.
6. **Bake the Cake:**
   - Pour the batter into the prepared cake pan(s) and smooth the top with a spatula.
   - Bake in the preheated oven for 25-30 minutes (for round pans) or 35-40 minutes (for a 9x13-inch pan), or until a toothpick inserted into the center comes out clean.
7. **Cool the Cake:**
   - Allow the cake to cool in the pan for about 10 minutes, then transfer it to a wire rack to cool completely.
8. **Prepare the Cream Cheese Frosting (Optional):**
   - In a medium bowl, beat the softened cream cheese and butter until smooth.
   - Gradually add the powdered sugar, beating until combined and smooth.
   - Mix in the vanilla extract. If the frosting is too thick, add milk or heavy cream a little at a time until it reaches the desired consistency.
9. **Frost and Serve:**
   - Once the cake is completely cooled, spread the cream cheese frosting evenly over the top and sides of the cake.
   - Decorate with a sprinkle of cinnamon or nutmeg if desired.
10. **Store:**
    - Store the cake in an airtight container in the refrigerator for up to 5 days. The cake can also be frozen for up to 3 months. Wrap it tightly in plastic wrap before freezing.

Tips

- **Pumpkin Puree:** Use pure pumpkin puree for the best flavor. Avoid pumpkin pie filling, which has added spices and sugar.
- **Spices:** Adjust the spice levels to taste. For a stronger spice flavor, increase the amount of cinnamon or other spices.
- **Frosting:** The cream cheese frosting adds a tangy sweetness that complements the pumpkin spice cake perfectly, but you can also use a simple glaze or enjoy the cake plain.

Pumpkin Spice Cake is a wonderful celebration of fall flavors. With its moist texture and aromatic spices, it's sure to be a hit at any gathering or as a comforting treat for yourself.

Maple Syrup Panna Cotta

Ingredients

- 1 cup heavy cream
- 1/2 cup whole milk
- 1/2 cup pure maple syrup
- 1/4 cup granulated sugar
- 1 envelope (2 1/4 teaspoons) unflavored gelatin
- 2 tablespoons water
- 1 teaspoon vanilla extract

Instructions

1. **Prepare the Gelatin:**
    - In a small bowl, sprinkle the gelatin over the water. Let it sit for 5-10 minutes to bloom, which means the gelatin will absorb the water and swell.
2. **Heat the Cream Mixture:**
    - In a medium saucepan, combine the heavy cream, whole milk, granulated sugar, and maple syrup. Heat over medium heat, stirring occasionally, until the mixture is warm and the sugar is dissolved. Do not let it boil.
3. **Dissolve the Gelatin:**
    - Remove the saucepan from the heat. Add the bloomed gelatin to the warm cream mixture, stirring until the gelatin is completely dissolved. Stir in the vanilla extract.
4. **Pour and Chill:**
    - Pour the mixture into individual serving glasses or ramekins. Allow it to cool slightly at room temperature.
    - Cover and refrigerate for at least 4 hours, or until the panna cotta is set and firm to the touch.
5. **Serve:**
    - Before serving, you can garnish the panna cotta with additional maple syrup, fresh berries, or a sprinkle of sea salt for extra flavor.

Tips

- **Gelatin:** Ensure that the gelatin is fully dissolved to avoid lumps in the panna cotta. If you encounter lumps, you can strain the mixture through a fine-mesh sieve before pouring it into the serving dishes.
- **Maple Syrup:** Use high-quality pure maple syrup for the best flavor. Imitation maple syrup will not provide the same depth of flavor.

- **Serving:** If you wish to unmold the panna cotta, lightly grease the ramekins or glasses with cooking spray before adding the mixture. To release, dip the bottoms of the ramekins briefly in warm water, then invert onto plates.

Maple Syrup Panna Cotta offers a luxurious and smooth texture with a delightful maple flavor, making it a perfect finish to any meal. Its simplicity and elegance ensure that it will be a hit with anyone who enjoys a refined dessert.

Chocolate and Maple Pots de Crème

Ingredients

- **1 cup heavy cream**
- **1 cup whole milk**
- **1/2 cup pure maple syrup**
- **4 ounces bittersweet chocolate** (finely chopped or in chips)
- **3 large egg yolks**
- **1/4 cup granulated sugar**
- **1/2 teaspoon vanilla extract**
- **Pinch of salt**

Instructions

1. **Preheat the Oven:**
   - Preheat your oven to 325°F (163°C).
2. **Heat Cream and Milk:**
   - In a medium saucepan, combine the heavy cream, whole milk, and maple syrup. Heat over medium heat, stirring occasionally, until the mixture is hot but not boiling. Remove from heat.
3. **Melt the Chocolate:**
   - Add the finely chopped bittersweet chocolate to the hot cream mixture. Let it sit for a minute to soften, then stir until the chocolate is completely melted and the mixture is smooth.
4. **Whisk Egg Yolks and Sugar:**
   - In a separate bowl, whisk together the egg yolks, granulated sugar, vanilla extract, and a pinch of salt until the mixture is pale and slightly thickened.
5. **Temper the Egg Mixture:**
   - Gradually add a small amount of the hot chocolate mixture to the egg yolks, whisking constantly to temper the eggs and prevent them from curdling.
   - Slowly pour the tempered egg yolk mixture back into the saucepan with the remaining chocolate mixture, whisking constantly.
6. **Strain and Pour:**
   - Strain the mixture through a fine-mesh sieve into a clean bowl to remove any curdled bits or impurities.
   - Divide the mixture evenly among 6-8 small ramekins or custard cups.
7. **Bake in a Water Bath:**
   - Place the ramekins in a baking dish and carefully pour hot water into the dish to come halfway up the sides of the ramekins (this creates a water bath, which helps the custards cook evenly).

- Bake in the preheated oven for 25-30 minutes, or until the pots de crème are just set but still slightly jiggly in the center.
8. **Cool and Chill:**
    - Remove the ramekins from the water bath and let them cool to room temperature. Once cooled, cover and refrigerate for at least 4 hours, or until well chilled.
9. **Serve:**
    - Serve the pots de crème chilled, garnished with a dollop of whipped cream, a drizzle of additional maple syrup, or a sprinkle of sea salt if desired.

Tips

- **Chocolate:** Use high-quality bittersweet chocolate for the best flavor. If you prefer a less intense chocolate flavor, you can use semisweet chocolate.
- **Water Bath:** Ensure the water bath does not splash into the ramekins, as this can cause the custard to become watery.
- **Chilling:** Allowing the pots de crème to chill for several hours ensures the flavors meld together and the texture becomes perfectly smooth.

Chocolate and Maple Pots de Crème offer a sophisticated balance of rich chocolate and sweet maple, making them an elegant and delightful choice for any dessert lover. Enjoy this creamy, indulgent treat as a special finish to your meal.

Maple Bacon Cupcakes

Ingredients

For the Maple Bacon Cupcakes:

- 1 1/2 cups all-purpose flour
- 1 teaspoon baking powder
- 1/2 teaspoon baking soda
- 1/4 teaspoon salt
- 1/2 cup unsalted butter (room temperature)
- 1/2 cup granulated sugar
- 1/2 cup packed light brown sugar
- 2 large eggs
- 1/2 cup pure maple syrup
- 1/2 cup whole milk
- 1 teaspoon vanilla extract
- 1/2 cup cooked bacon (crumbled, preferably from about 6-8 strips)

For the Maple Bacon Frosting:

- 1/2 cup unsalted butter (room temperature)
- 1/4 cup pure maple syrup
- 2 cups powdered sugar
- 1/2 teaspoon vanilla extract
- 1-2 tablespoons milk or heavy cream (if needed for consistency)
- 1/4 cup cooked bacon (crumbled, for garnish)

Instructions

1. **Prepare the Oven and Pan:**
   - Preheat your oven to 350°F (175°C).
   - Line a 12-cup muffin pan with cupcake liners.
2. **Mix Dry Ingredients:**
   - In a medium bowl, whisk together the flour, baking powder, baking soda, and salt. Set aside.
3. **Cream Butter and Sugars:**
   - In a large mixing bowl, use an electric mixer to beat the butter until creamy.
   - Add the granulated sugar and brown sugar, and beat until light and fluffy.
4. **Add Eggs and Flavorings:**
   - Add the eggs one at a time, beating well after each addition.
   - Mix in the maple syrup, milk, and vanilla extract until combined.
5. **Combine Dry and Wet Ingredients:**

- Gradually add the dry ingredients to the butter mixture, mixing just until combined.
- Fold in the crumbled bacon.
6. **Fill and Bake:**
    - Divide the batter evenly among the cupcake liners, filling each about 2/3 full.
    - Bake in the preheated oven for 18-22 minutes, or until a toothpick inserted into the center comes out clean.
7. **Cool the Cupcakes:**
    - Allow the cupcakes to cool in the pan for 5 minutes, then transfer them to a wire rack to cool completely before frosting.
8. **Prepare the Frosting:**
    - In a medium bowl, beat the butter until creamy.
    - Gradually add the powdered sugar, beating until smooth.
    - Mix in the maple syrup and vanilla extract.
    - If the frosting is too thick, add milk or heavy cream a little at a time until it reaches the desired consistency.
9. **Frost and Garnish:**
    - Frost the cooled cupcakes with the maple bacon frosting using a piping bag or spatula.
    - Garnish with additional crumbled bacon on top of each cupcake.
10. **Serve and Enjoy:**
    - Enjoy the cupcakes fresh, or store them in an airtight container at room temperature for up to 3 days.

Tips

- **Bacon:** For best results, use thick-cut bacon and cook it until crispy. Drain on paper towels before crumbling.
- **Maple Syrup:** Use pure maple syrup for the most authentic flavor. Avoid imitation syrup for the best results.
- **Frosting Consistency:** Adjust the thickness of the frosting by adding more powdered sugar if too thin or more milk/cream if too thick.

Maple Bacon Cupcakes offer a deliciously unexpected combination of flavors that will surely be a hit at any event. The sweet maple cake paired with the salty crunch of bacon creates a unique and irresistible dessert experience.

Strawberry Rhubarb Pie

Ingredients

For the Pie Crust:

- **2 1/2 cups all-purpose flour**
- **1 cup unsalted butter** (chilled and cut into small pieces)
- **1/4 cup granulated sugar**
- **1/4 teaspoon salt**
- **1/4 to 1/2 cup ice water** (as needed)

For the Strawberry Rhubarb Filling:

- **2 cups fresh strawberries** (hulled and sliced)
- **2 cups fresh rhubarb** (cut into 1/2-inch pieces)
- **1 cup granulated sugar**
- **1/4 cup cornstarch**
- **1/4 teaspoon salt**
- **1 tablespoon lemon juice**
- **1 teaspoon vanilla extract**
- **1/2 teaspoon ground cinnamon** (optional)
- **1 tablespoon unsalted butter** (cut into small pieces, for dotting)

Instructions

1. **Prepare the Pie Crust:**
    - In a large bowl, whisk together the flour, sugar, and salt.
    - Add the chilled butter pieces and use a pastry cutter or your fingers to work the butter into the flour until the mixture resembles coarse crumbs with pea-sized butter pieces.
    - Gradually add the ice water, one tablespoon at a time, mixing until the dough just comes together. Avoid overworking the dough.
    - Divide the dough into two discs, wrap in plastic wrap, and refrigerate for at least 1 hour or overnight.
2. **Prepare the Filling:**
    - In a large bowl, combine the strawberries, rhubarb, granulated sugar, cornstarch, salt, lemon juice, vanilla extract, and cinnamon (if using). Mix well and set aside to let the juices combine.
3. **Assemble the Pie:**
    - Preheat your oven to 425°F (220°C).
    - On a lightly floured surface, roll out one of the dough discs into a 12-inch circle. Transfer it to a 9-inch pie dish, trimming any excess dough.

- Pour the strawberry rhubarb filling into the pie crust, spreading it evenly.
- Dot the filling with small pieces of butter.
- Roll out the second dough disc and place it over the filling. You can either cover the pie with a full crust, or cut the dough into strips to create a lattice pattern. Trim and crimp the edges of the crust.
- Cut a few small slits in the top crust if using a full crust, to allow steam to escape.

4. **Bake the Pie:**
   - Place the pie on a baking sheet to catch any drips and bake in the preheated oven for 45-55 minutes, or until the crust is golden brown and the filling is bubbling.
   - If the edges of the crust start to brown too quickly, cover them with aluminum foil to prevent burning.

5. **Cool and Serve:**
   - Allow the pie to cool on a wire rack for at least 2 hours before serving. This cooling period helps the filling set properly.
   - Serve the pie as is, or with a scoop of vanilla ice cream or a dollop of whipped cream.

Tips

- **Rhubarb:** Fresh rhubarb is ideal, but if you're using frozen rhubarb, make sure to thaw and drain it well to avoid excess moisture in the filling.
- **Crust:** For a more tender crust, handle the dough as little as possible and keep the ingredients as cold as you can.
- **Thickening:** The cornstarch helps thicken the filling, but if you prefer a firmer filling, you can increase the amount slightly.

Strawberry Rhubarb Pie is a delightful blend of sweet and tart flavors, wrapped in a buttery, flaky crust. This classic dessert is a wonderful choice for showcasing seasonal produce and making any occasion a little sweeter.

Oatmeal Raisin Cookies with Maple Glaze

Ingredients

For the Oatmeal Raisin Cookies:

- **1 cup unsalted butter** (room temperature)
- **1 cup granulated sugar**
- **1 cup packed light brown sugar**
- **2 large eggs**
- **1 teaspoon vanilla extract**
- **1 1/2 cups all-purpose flour**
- **1 teaspoon baking soda**
- **1/2 teaspoon ground cinnamon**
- **1/4 teaspoon salt**
- **3 cups old-fashioned oats**
- **1 cup raisins**

For the Maple Glaze:

- **1 cup powdered sugar**
- **2 tablespoons pure maple syrup**
- **1-2 tablespoons milk** (as needed for consistency)
- **1/2 teaspoon vanilla extract**

Instructions

1. **Prepare the Oven:**
   - Preheat your oven to 350°F (175°C).
   - Line two baking sheets with parchment paper or silicone baking mats.
2. **Make the Cookie Dough:**
   - In a large bowl, use an electric mixer to cream the butter, granulated sugar, and brown sugar until light and fluffy.
   - Add the eggs one at a time, beating well after each addition. Mix in the vanilla extract.
   - In a separate bowl, whisk together the flour, baking soda, cinnamon, and salt.
   - Gradually add the dry ingredients to the wet ingredients, mixing just until combined.
   - Stir in the oats and raisins until evenly distributed.
3. **Shape and Bake the Cookies:**
   - Drop rounded tablespoons of dough onto the prepared baking sheets, spacing them about 2 inches apart.

- Bake in the preheated oven for 10-12 minutes, or until the edges are golden brown and the centers are set. The cookies will continue to firm up as they cool.
- Allow the cookies to cool on the baking sheets for 5 minutes before transferring them to wire racks to cool completely.

4. **Prepare the Maple Glaze:**
   - In a medium bowl, whisk together the powdered sugar, maple syrup, vanilla extract, and 1 tablespoon of milk.
   - If the glaze is too thick, add additional milk, one teaspoon at a time, until you reach a drizzling consistency.
5. **Glaze the Cookies:**
   - Once the cookies are completely cooled, drizzle the maple glaze over the tops of the cookies using a spoon or a piping bag.
   - Let the glaze set for a few minutes before serving.
6. **Serve and Enjoy:**
   - Enjoy the cookies fresh or store them in an airtight container at room temperature for up to a week.

Tips

- **Butter:** Make sure the butter is at room temperature to achieve a smooth and creamy cookie dough.
- **Oats:** Use old-fashioned oats for the best texture. Quick oats can be used but may result in a slightly different texture.
- **Glaze:** The maple glaze can be adjusted in sweetness and consistency by adding more powdered sugar or milk as needed.

Oatmeal Raisin Cookies with Maple Glaze are a delicious and unique take on a classic favorite. The combination of hearty oats, sweet raisins, and the rich flavor of maple glaze makes these cookies an irresistible treat that's perfect for any occasion.

Butterscotch Maple Blondies

Ingredients

- **1 cup unsalted butter** (room temperature)
- **1 cup packed light brown sugar**
- **1/2 cup granulated sugar**
- **1/2 cup pure maple syrup**
- **2 large eggs**
- **1 teaspoon vanilla extract**
- **2 1/4 cups all-purpose flour**
- **1 teaspoon baking powder**
- **1/2 teaspoon salt**
- **1 cup butterscotch chips**

Instructions

1. **Prepare the Oven:**
   - Preheat your oven to 350°F (175°C).
   - Line a 9x13-inch baking pan with parchment paper, leaving an overhang for easy removal, or lightly grease the pan.
2. **Make the Blondie Batter:**
   - In a large mixing bowl, use an electric mixer to cream the butter, brown sugar, and granulated sugar until light and fluffy.
   - Beat in the maple syrup, eggs, and vanilla extract until well combined.
   - In a separate bowl, whisk together the flour, baking powder, and salt.
   - Gradually add the dry ingredients to the wet ingredients, mixing just until combined.
   - Fold in the butterscotch chips.
3. **Bake the Blondies:**
   - Spread the batter evenly into the prepared baking pan.
   - Bake in the preheated oven for 25-30 minutes, or until the top is golden brown and a toothpick inserted into the center comes out with only a few moist crumbs.
   - Be careful not to overbake, as the blondies will continue to firm up as they cool.
4. **Cool and Cut:**
   - Allow the blondies to cool in the pan on a wire rack for about 15 minutes.
   - Use the parchment paper overhang to lift the blondies out of the pan and place them on the wire rack to cool completely.
   - Once cooled, cut into squares or bars.
5. **Serve and Enjoy:**
   - Enjoy the blondies on their own, or serve them warm with a scoop of vanilla ice cream for an extra indulgent treat.

Tips

- **Butter:** Ensure the butter is at room temperature for a smooth and creamy batter.
- **Maple Syrup:** Use high-quality pure maple syrup for the best flavor. Imitation syrup will not provide the same depth of taste.
- **Butterscotch Chips:** For a more intense butterscotch flavor, you can slightly increase the amount of chips or add a handful of chopped nuts for added texture.

Butterscotch Maple Blondies are a rich and delicious dessert that combines the best of butterscotch and maple flavors. Their soft, chewy texture and sweet, buttery taste make them a perfect treat for any occasion, whether you're enjoying a quiet afternoon at home or entertaining guests.

Pecan Pie Bars

Ingredients

For the Crust:

- **1 cup all-purpose flour**
- **1/4 cup granulated sugar**
- **1/4 teaspoon salt**
- **1/2 cup unsalted butter** (cold and cut into small pieces)

For the Pecan Filling:

- **1 cup light corn syrup**
- **1 cup packed brown sugar**
- **1/2 cup unsalted butter** (melted)
- **3 large eggs**
- **1 teaspoon vanilla extract**
- **1/4 teaspoon salt**
- **2 cups pecan halves**

Instructions

1. **Prepare the Oven and Pan:**
   - Preheat your oven to 350°F (175°C).
   - Line an 8x8-inch baking pan with parchment paper, leaving an overhang on the sides for easy removal, or lightly grease the pan.
2. **Make the Crust:**
   - In a medium bowl, whisk together the flour, sugar, and salt.
   - Cut in the cold butter using a pastry cutter or your fingers until the mixture resembles coarse crumbs.
   - Press the mixture evenly into the bottom of the prepared baking pan to form the crust.
   - Bake in the preheated oven for 10 minutes, or until lightly golden.
3. **Prepare the Pecan Filling:**
   - While the crust is baking, in a large bowl, whisk together the corn syrup, brown sugar, melted butter, eggs, vanilla extract, and salt until smooth.
   - Stir in the pecan halves until evenly coated.
4. **Assemble and Bake:**
   - Pour the pecan filling over the partially baked crust, spreading it evenly.
   - Return to the oven and bake for an additional 30-35 minutes, or until the filling is set and the top is golden brown. The filling should be slightly firm to the touch.
5. **Cool and Cut:**

- Allow the bars to cool completely in the pan on a wire rack before cutting into squares.
- Use the parchment paper overhang to lift the bars out of the pan for easier cutting.

6. **Serve and Enjoy:**
   - Serve the pecan pie bars at room temperature or chilled. They can be stored in an airtight container at room temperature for up to 1 week or refrigerated for longer storage.

Tips

- **Butter:** Ensure the butter is cold when making the crust to achieve a flaky texture.
- **Corn Syrup:** Light corn syrup is traditional for pecan pie, but you can use dark corn syrup for a richer flavor if preferred.
- **Pecans:** Toast the pecans lightly before adding them to the filling for a deeper, nuttier flavor.

Pecan Pie Bars provide all the delicious flavors of traditional pecan pie in a convenient, easy-to-serve form. Their buttery crust and gooey pecan filling make them a perfect dessert for any occasion, bringing the warmth and comfort of pecan pie to your table.

Maple-Almond Cake

Ingredients

For the Cake:

- 1 cup almond flour
- 1 cup all-purpose flour
- 1/2 cup granulated sugar
- 1/2 cup packed light brown sugar
- 1/2 cup unsalted butter (room temperature)
- 1/2 cup pure maple syrup
- 3 large eggs
- 1 teaspoon vanilla extract
- 1 teaspoon baking powder
- 1/4 teaspoon baking soda
- 1/4 teaspoon salt

For the Maple Almond Glaze:

- 1/2 cup powdered sugar
- 2 tablespoons pure maple syrup
- 1-2 tablespoons milk (as needed for consistency)
- 1/4 cup sliced almonds (for garnish)

Instructions

1. **Prepare the Oven and Pan:**
   - Preheat your oven to 350°F (175°C).
   - Grease and flour an 8-inch round cake pan or line it with parchment paper.
2. **Make the Cake Batter:**
   - In a large mixing bowl, cream together the butter, granulated sugar, and brown sugar until light and fluffy.
   - Beat in the eggs one at a time, ensuring each is fully incorporated before adding the next.
   - Mix in the maple syrup and vanilla extract until well combined.
   - In a separate bowl, whisk together the almond flour, all-purpose flour, baking powder, baking soda, and salt.
   - Gradually add the dry ingredients to the wet ingredients, mixing just until combined.
3. **Bake the Cake:**
   - Pour the batter into the prepared cake pan and spread it evenly.

- Bake in the preheated oven for 30-35 minutes, or until a toothpick inserted into the center comes out clean.
- Allow the cake to cool in the pan for 10 minutes before transferring it to a wire rack to cool completely.
4. **Prepare the Maple Almond Glaze:**
    - In a small bowl, whisk together the powdered sugar, maple syrup, and 1 tablespoon of milk.
    - If the glaze is too thick, add more milk, a little at a time, until it reaches a drizzling consistency.
5. **Glaze the Cake:**
    - Once the cake has cooled completely, drizzle the maple glaze over the top, allowing it to drip down the sides.
    - Sprinkle the sliced almonds over the glaze for added texture and decoration.
6. **Serve and Enjoy:**
    - Slice the cake and serve at room temperature. The cake can be stored in an airtight container at room temperature for up to 4 days or refrigerated for longer storage.

Tips

- **Almond Flour:** For best results, use finely ground almond flour. This will help achieve a smooth texture in the cake.
- **Maple Syrup:** Use high-quality pure maple syrup for the most authentic and flavorful result.
- **Glaze:** Adjust the consistency of the glaze by adding more milk or powdered sugar as needed.

Maple-Almond Cake is a delightful dessert that combines the comforting flavors of almond and maple in a moist, tender cake. Its elegant appearance and rich flavor make it a perfect choice for special occasions or as a luxurious treat to enjoy with loved ones.

Apple Maple Muffins

Ingredients

For the Muffins:

- 1 1/2 cups all-purpose flour
- 1/2 cup whole wheat flour (optional for added texture)
- 1/2 cup granulated sugar
- 1/4 cup packed light brown sugar
- 2 teaspoons baking powder
- 1/2 teaspoon baking soda
- 1/2 teaspoon ground cinnamon
- 1/4 teaspoon ground nutmeg
- 1/4 teaspoon salt
- 1/2 cup unsalted butter (melted and slightly cooled)
- 1/2 cup pure maple syrup
- 2 large eggs
- 1 teaspoon vanilla extract
- 1 cup diced apples (peeled and cored; use a firm variety like Honeycrisp or Granny Smith)

For the Topping (Optional):

- 2 tablespoons granulated sugar
- 1/2 teaspoon ground cinnamon

Instructions

1. **Prepare the Oven and Muffin Tin:**
   - Preheat your oven to 375°F (190°C).
   - Line a 12-cup muffin tin with paper liners or lightly grease the cups.
2. **Mix the Dry Ingredients:**
   - In a large bowl, whisk together the all-purpose flour, whole wheat flour (if using), granulated sugar, brown sugar, baking powder, baking soda, cinnamon, nutmeg, and salt.
3. **Prepare the Wet Ingredients:**
   - In a separate bowl, combine the melted butter, maple syrup, eggs, and vanilla extract. Mix until well combined.
4. **Combine and Fold:**
   - Pour the wet ingredients into the dry ingredients and stir until just combined. Avoid over-mixing.
   - Gently fold in the diced apples.

5. **Fill and Top:**
   - Divide the batter evenly among the 12 muffin cups, filling each about 2/3 full.
   - If desired, mix the granulated sugar and cinnamon for the topping and sprinkle a small amount over each muffin.
6. **Bake:**
   - Bake in the preheated oven for 20-25 minutes, or until a toothpick inserted into the center comes out clean and the tops are golden brown.
7. **Cool and Serve:**
   - Allow the muffins to cool in the tin for 5 minutes before transferring them to a wire rack to cool completely.
   - Serve warm or at room temperature.

Tips

- **Apples:** For the best texture, use firm apples that hold their shape well during baking.
- **Maple Syrup:** Use pure maple syrup for the most authentic flavor. Artificial syrup can affect the taste and texture of the muffins.
- **Texture:** For extra moisture and a slightly different texture, you can add a tablespoon of sour cream or yogurt to the batter.

Apple Maple Muffins offer a delicious combination of flavors and textures, with the sweetness of maple syrup complementing the tartness of fresh apples. These muffins are a wonderful way to start your day or enjoy as a delightful snack.

Maple Marshmallow Rice Krispies Treats

Ingredients

- **6 cups Rice Krispies cereal**
- **4 tablespoons unsalted butter**
- **1 package (10 oz) mini marshmallows** (about 4 cups)
- **1/2 cup pure maple syrup**
- **1/2 teaspoon vanilla extract** (optional)
- **Pinch of salt**

Instructions

1. **Prepare the Pan:**
    - Lightly grease a 9x13-inch baking pan or line it with parchment paper.
2. **Melt the Butter and Marshmallows:**
    - In a large saucepan, melt the butter over low heat.
    - Once melted, add the mini marshmallows, stirring continuously until completely melted and smooth.
3. **Incorporate Maple Syrup:**
    - Stir in the pure maple syrup and a pinch of salt until well combined. If using, add the vanilla extract and mix thoroughly.
4. **Combine with Cereal:**
    - Remove the saucepan from the heat and add the Rice Krispies cereal to the marshmallow mixture.
    - Stir gently but thoroughly until the cereal is evenly coated with the marshmallow mixture.
5. **Transfer to Pan:**
    - Pour the mixture into the prepared baking pan. Using a spatula or your hands (greased to prevent sticking), press the mixture evenly and firmly into the pan.
6. **Cool and Cut:**
    - Allow the treats to cool completely in the pan at room temperature before cutting into squares or bars.
    - For quicker cooling, you can place the pan in the refrigerator for about 30 minutes.
7. **Serve and Enjoy:**
    - Once cooled and cut, serve the Maple Marshmallow Rice Krispies Treats. They can be stored in an airtight container at room temperature for up to a week.

Tips

- **Butter:** Ensure that the butter is melted gently over low heat to prevent burning.
- **Maple Syrup:** Use pure maple syrup for the best flavor. The syrup adds a natural sweetness and a hint of maple that complements the marshmallows.
- **Mixing:** Be gentle when mixing the cereal into the marshmallow mixture to avoid crushing the cereal too much.

Maple Marshmallow Rice Krispies Treats are a deliciously sweet and crunchy treat with a unique maple twist. Their gooey, marshmallowy texture combined with the warm flavor of maple syrup makes them a delightful snack for both kids and adults.

Hazelnut Maple Tart

Ingredients

For the Crust:

- **1 1/2 cups all-purpose flour**
- **1/2 cup ground hazelnuts**
- **1/4 cup granulated sugar**
- **1/4 teaspoon salt**
- **1/2 cup unsalted butter** (cold and cut into small pieces)
- **1 large egg yolk**
- **2 tablespoons cold water**

For the Filling:

- **1 cup toasted hazelnuts** (coarsely chopped)
- **1/2 cup pure maple syrup**
- **1/4 cup granulated sugar**
- **1/4 cup unsalted butter** (melted)
- **2 large eggs**
- **1 teaspoon vanilla extract**
- **1/4 teaspoon salt**

For Garnish (Optional):

- **Whole toasted hazelnuts**
- **Powdered sugar** (for dusting)

Instructions

1. **Prepare the Crust:**
   - Preheat your oven to 350°F (175°C).
   - In a food processor, combine the flour, ground hazelnuts, granulated sugar, and salt. Pulse to blend.
   - Add the cold butter and pulse until the mixture resembles coarse crumbs.
   - In a small bowl, mix the egg yolk and cold water. Add this to the food processor and pulse until the dough starts to come together.
   - Transfer the dough to a lightly floured surface and gently press it into a disk. Roll out the dough to fit a 9-inch tart pan with a removable bottom. Press the dough into the pan, trimming the edges.
   - Prick the bottom of the crust with a fork and freeze for 15 minutes.
2. **Pre-Bake the Crust:**

- Bake the crust in the preheated oven for 15 minutes, or until lightly golden.
- Remove from the oven and let it cool slightly.
3. **Prepare the Filling:**
    - In a large bowl, whisk together the toasted hazelnuts, maple syrup, granulated sugar, melted butter, eggs, vanilla extract, and salt until well combined.
    - Pour the filling into the pre-baked crust.
4. **Bake the Tart:**
    - Bake the tart in the oven for 25-30 minutes, or until the filling is set and slightly puffed, and the top is golden brown.
    - Allow the tart to cool completely in the pan on a wire rack before removing it.
5. **Garnish and Serve:**
    - Once cooled, garnish with whole toasted hazelnuts and a light dusting of powdered sugar, if desired.
    - Serve the tart at room temperature or chilled.
6. **Store:**
    - The Hazelnut Maple Tart can be stored in an airtight container at room temperature for up to 3 days or refrigerated for up to 1 week.

Tips

- **Hazelnuts:** Toast the hazelnuts lightly in the oven or on a skillet before using to enhance their flavor.
- **Crust:** Make sure the crust is well-chilled before baking to prevent it from shrinking.
- **Filling:** If the filling bubbles up too much while baking, you can cover it with aluminum foil and continue baking until it is set.

Hazelnut Maple Tart is a luxurious dessert that combines the nutty richness of hazelnuts with the sweet depth of maple syrup. Its elegant presentation and sophisticated flavors make it a perfect choice for holiday gatherings, special occasions, or simply as a special treat to enjoy with loved ones.

www.ingramcontent.com/pod-product-compliance
Lightning Source LLC
LaVergne TN
LVHW081556060526
838201LV00054B/1912